# THE NON-HUMORIST'S HANDBOOK

## How to Easily Add Humor to Your Speeches

Originally Titled: *A Handbook for Non-Humorists*

# BRIAN WOOLF

**The Non-Humorist's Handbook:**
**How to Easily Add Humor to Speeches**

**ISBN-13: 978-09632025-6-7** (paperback)

Library of Congress Control Number: 2017917113
Originally titled: *A Handbook for Non-Humorists*

1. Humor. 2. Public Speaking 3. Communications

Published by Teal Books
*brianwoolf@speakers-toolbox.com*

Cover Design: Amy Tedder, *www.atyourdesign.com*

ALSO BY BRIAN WOOLF
*Shrinking the Corporate Waistline*
*Measured Marketing: A Tool to Shape Food Store Strategy*
*Customer Specific Marketing: The New Power in Retailing*
*Loyalty Marketing: The Second Act*
*The Speaker's Toolbox: 47 Tools to Build Better Speeches*

*Available at Amazon.com and leading booksellers*

For quantity discounts, please contact the author at:
*brianwoolf@speakers-toolbox.com*

First edition January 2018

Printed in the United States of America

*To Marie,*
*my loving, patient wife*
*of over 40 years*

# Contents

Introduction    1

## Part I

**Humor Help for Speakers**    3

Twists    5

Asides    37

Putdowns    55

Exaggeration    81

*Make TAPE Your MATE*

## Part II

**Humor Help for Chairmen**    107

Chair – For All Events    109

Chair – For Toastmaster Events    133

Superscripts Index    144

About the Author    148

# Introduction

## Why this book?

For too many years I was a Non-Humorist. I was a straight-laced, analytically-minded accountant who saw fellow Toastmasters® using humor in their speeches, seemingly without effort, and wished I could, too. Since I didn't know how, my early attempts generally failed. However, given the way my mind works, I decided to analyze humor to see if there was a way, a method, a path, that would help me at least crack a smile or, perhaps, even evoke a light laugh. My journey took a lot of time yet I eventually succeeded. I now comfortably trigger smiles and laughter before audiences of all sizes and when chairing large meetings. This book covers the approach I learned.

Over the past 50 years, I have observed that the majority of people appear to be Non-Humorists, many wanting to change their status. This book is written for them. It explains the four simple, easy ways to confidently add humor when speaking. And the more often one does, the more comfortable one becomes. It's a journey that has no end because once attuned to simple, humorous ideas, new ones just keep appearing.

## Is this book for you?

Do you feel that:

- Speaking humorously is beyond you—but you wish it wasn't?
- You are uncomfortable or just plain shy about using humor in speeches?
- You don't know where to begin even if you wanted to add humor to your speeches?

If you nod your head in agreement with any of the above, this book is for you. It will show you how to easily inject humor into speeches. No, it won't turn you into an over-night success as a stand-up comic—but it will put you on a path, guided by many examples, which gives you the comfort and confidence to create humor when giving a speech.

There are a variety of ways to spark laughter as a speaker. This book deals with the four easiest, based upon viewing and studying many hundreds of speeches and reading innumerable books on humor.

The four easiest humor tools for speeches are:

**T**wists
**A**sides
**P**utdowns
**E**xaggeration

They succeed, because they:

- Are simple to understand and use.
- Are easy to create, remember, and deliver.
- Have the element of surprise, the foundation stone of humor.
- Generate smiles and laughter which builds bonds with audiences.
- Have a low risk of failure, and if one does, it's over-looked and quickly forgotten.

1

Each tool is covered in a three-part framework — 1) definition complete with explanation; 2) lessons and comments from a platform speaker; and 3) a wide-ranging selection of examples showing its use in many circumstances. After each example, space is provided to let you pencil in notes, ideas, and other examples that pop into your mind as you read.

## A second reason for the book

If you are interested in adding humor to your speeches, then you will also most likely welcome humor help on those occasions when invited to be the chairman, toastmaster, or emcee of a large meeting, conference, or contest. The formal, routine ("dry") part of such meetings is easy; it's the sprinkling of lightness and levity throughout the meeting that's the challenge.

As it's difficult to find such helpful material, the second part of this book provides it in the form of quips, quotes, witticisms, observations, and one-liners. The material is covered in two chapters: the first is a collection that works for (or is adaptable to) almost any meeting, while the second provides helpful material specifically for chairmen of Toastmasters meetings with its unique vernacular, although non-Toastmasters will gain from it, too. The second chapter will be of particular interest to members of organizations with their own lingo, such as Rotary, Lions, and Kiwanis.

If you attend large meetings, you will know that well-placed one-liners by the meeting chairman not only add smiles and laughter to the meeting but also to the chairman's esteem in the eyes of the audience.

## One caveat

There are many attributed quotations in this book. Speaking etiquette tells us that if we ever wish to use such a quote, certainly do so, but reference the source. However, if an idea is triggered by a quote and we personalize it or express it in some way that is clearly different from the original, then acknowledgement is not necessary.

## How to read this book

Rather than reading it cover to cover, my suggestion is to first read the brief introductory pages for each chapter to familiarize yourself with each tool. Then flit from chapter to chapter scanning the examples, swooping down to read, and munching on those that resonate (but don't laugh when your mouth is full!) After that overview, go back to the sections you enjoyed most to read more, and start experimenting with, and using, those particular tools. Generously jot down your own ideas: this is *your* humor handbook.

*Brian Woolf*
*Greenville, South Carolina*
*January 14, 2018*

# Part I

# Humor Help for Speakers

## Twists
Definition & Explanation     5
Lessons from a Leader: Jock Elliott     7
Examples     9

## Asides
Definition & Explanation     37
Lessons from a Leader: Kelly Swanson     38
Examples     39

## Putdowns
Definition & Explanation     55
Lessons from a Leader: Darren LaCroix     56
Examples     61

## Exaggeration
Definition & Explanation     81
Lessons from a Leader: Randy Harvey     82
Examples     83

*Make TAPE Your MATE*

# Twists

One of the easiest ways to create smiles and laughter in speeches is to use a Twist. My favorite example comes from the 2001 World Championship of Public Speaking®:

*Gentlemen, you have no idea of the power of a love letter—until your wife intercepts one!*

The above sentence has an elegantly simple, two-step structure: Short statement (set-up)—Surprise redirection (punchline). The speaker, J A Gamache, had us moving in one direction and then—Wham!—we were redirected in a surprising and completely different direction which triggered a wave of loud laughter throughout the huge ballroom.

A Twist, by definition, comprises one or more setup steps that take listeners' minds down a particular path which, all of a sudden, changes in an unexpected and amusing direction. The setup(s) comes first; the Twist (punchline, punch clause, or punch word) is always last.

**Two-part Twists** are brief, easy to build, and easy to deliver as these examples show:

*My New Year's resolution was to lose 10 pounds—I have only 15 to go.*

*Now where was I—before I rudely interrupted myself?*

*My plane left at 5:25—and I didn't.*

Twists generally generate smiles and laughter. And, when they don't, the downside is minimal. You just carry on with your speech; no one notices as they would if you had instead given a (longer) funny story that bombed.

Two-step Twists are, therefore, the perfect entry point for Non-Humorists to start the process of injecting humor into their speeches. Although two-step Twists are popular and widespread, Twists can be of any length.

**Three-step Twists** are similar to two-step Twists, but with an extra set-up statement. Their structure is: (1) Base statement; (2) Supporting or elaborating statement; and (3) Surprise Redirection. Examples of three-step Twists include:

*When I was 22, I got a job as a hydration specialist—a bartender* [JL^]

*Some great motivational speakers assure us that we become what we think about. If that were true—at 20 I would've been a svelte blond.* [JN^]

*By working faithfully eight hours a day, you may eventually get to be boss—and then work twelve hours a day.* [RF]

Two- and three-step Twists are common because of their brevity, simple construction, and low risk.

Occasionally, you will have the pleasure hearing a speaker delivering a clever four (or more) step Twist, like these:

### 4-Step Twist

*No cars, no stoplights, no pedestrians—NO LAWSUITS!* [DW+]
[Speaker explaining selection of a school parking lot to teach his daughter to drive.]

### 4-Step Twist

*I'll bet you're all like Mark Twain who said:*
*I've received many compliments in my life.*
*Was embarrassed by all of them—*
*They were all far too short!* [BW]

### 5-Step Twist

*I showed my mother my report card.*
*It was my worst ever.*
*She smiled.*
*"I'm proud of you son—*
*I can tell from your grades you don't cheat"* [JB^]

### Vignette Twist

As your Twisting confidence and competence grows, you will experiment with Twists of all lengths and even possibly create a story or vignette that ends in a Twist as does the following. The two back-to-back Twists that ended this speech earned Jay Nodine his fourth consecutive Humorous Speech title in Toastmasters District 37 (North Carolina). Jay was a true Twist Meister—and a wonderful friend and mentor to many.

*Doc, so are you saying*
*Nothing is wrong with my heart???*
*Mr. Nodine, I can safely say*
*Your heart will last—as long as you do!!!*

*Well then, I asked—Do you think I will live to be 80?*
*He asked—Do you smoke or drink in excess?*
*Oh no, I said.*
*He asked—Do you eat red meat?*
*I shook my head, Noooo.*
*He asked—Do you drive fast cars—and chase loose women?*
*No, I said—I don't do any of those things.*
*He said———Then why do you care???!!!*

## Lessons from Jock Elliott

Jock Elliott (www.jockelliott.com) is a popular, well-known World Champion Speaker. Over a 22-year period (1990-2011), on six occasions Jock earned a spot as one of Toastmasters 10 finalists for the World Championship (in '90, '93, '94, '06, '08, and '11, when he finally won)—making him one of the most persistent and inspirational contestants in the contest's history. Over the years, he also wrote the most contest speeches!

Jock plays with words and phrases as though they are putty. So, I sought his thoughts on how he uses Twists, from two-step to multi-step. He suggested that you, the reader, would benefit by seeing Twists in their surrounding speech context, and he has kindly provided that. Here are three of his many Twists that have amused and delighted global audiences.

## From "Just So Lucky," World Champion Winning Speech, 2011

*Oh, of course, we've had our differences, just like every family.*
*But I'm just so lucky because we got over those.*
*And if you can't shout at your brother and sister, well, who can you shout at?*
*And blood is thicker than water—and no-one is thicker than my brother.*

*Jock's comment:* Here I use the title for the second time in the speech. This is deliberate as some people have bad memories of family, and the first two sentences acknowledge that, and allow me and them to move on. Also, I have two spots of humor in this paragraph since there hasn't been any humor so far and I wanted to lighten the tone. I also close this section with a punch line. [Jock is saying he needed a humor injection so he deliberately crafted and added a simple but, memorable, two-step Twist.]

## Opening to "Que Sera," World Champion Contest Speech, 1994

*When I was just a little boy*
*I asked my mother*
*"What will I be?*
*Will I be handsome?*
*Will I be rich?"*
*Here's what she said to me.*
*She said—*
*'No.'*

*Jock's comment:* This 8-step Twist not only exploits the audience's knowledge of the song, and hence their expectations, but also leads into a three-part development towards the theme of the speech that also exploits the song and speech title. [Note: Jock's surprise Twist "No", after the well-known song's buildup, triggered laughter, relaxation, and a positive feeling towards him among the audience, making them look forward to hearing more of what he was going to say.]

## From "Five Smooth Stones," Semifinal Winning Speech, 1996

*All of us have seen a member of the opposite sex naked*
*And not closed our eyes—*
*That's called **curiosity**.*
*Jimmy Carter took a fancy to someone*
*Who was not his to fancy—*
*That's called **fantasy**.*
*He talked about it on national TV—*
*That's called **stupidity**.*
*Then his wife heard about it—*
*And that's called **catastrophe**.*
*And some of us may even have taken things to their logical conclusion*
*As Bill Clinton did*
*And that's the millstone—*
*Called **Lewinsky**.*

*Jock's comment:* In this instance, each punch word has a similar sounding last sylla-ble, and is polysyllabic as well, and each punch word is also prefaced by "called..." to highlight the label. The ultimate twist relies on each preceding judgmental label being both correct and slightly tragi-comic but the last one is a pure play on words, exploit-ing the last syllable. In each of these three examples, the use of pause is critical. [Note: The multi-step buildup here of some well-known images, with rhythmic descriptors, had the audience enthralled, so that when the surprise Twist at the end was deliv-ered, it triggered huge laughter. I know. I was there. As the laughter subsided, David Brooks (the 1990 World Champion Speaker) quietly whispered to me, "I believe that just won Jock the contest." It did, securing Jock a slot in the World's Final Ten Con-test several days later.]

## Comment

When reading your speech drafts, keep asking yourself which lines might be "twistable." Play with them. Test them.

To seed your mind with helpful ideas for this process, what follows is a very extensive array of Twists. They are drawn from attributed and unattributed sources, from scrib-bled notes and speeches over many years.

Examples that resonate with you can be used in three ways. Use the Twist in a speech, acknowledging its source (if known). Take the nub of the Twist's idea and create a distinctly different one, personalized in some way to you, where you live, or to your speech. Or simply welcome into your mind the new ideas triggered by the quotes. Over time, you'll find yourself doing all three. Enjoy the journey.

# Twists ~ Examples

Hospitality is the art of making guests feel like they're at home—and you wish they were.

Hallmark just announced an economy card—it's for those who don't deserve the very best. ~DB+

The tragedy is that the most knowledgeable people who should be in Congress don't have the time—they're too busy cutting hair and driving taxis. GB

Happiness is having a large, loving, caring, close-knit family—in another city. GB

Don't worry about avoiding temptation—as you grow older it will avoid you. WC

Somewhere on this globe, every 10 seconds, there is a woman giving birth to a child—she has to be found and stopped!!! SL

I found my husband on Match.com. At first no one liked him. Now, 10 years later—I understand why. SK^

Harry Truman's mother-in-law publicly predicted he'd lose re-election. Only time in history a mother-in-law has ever been wrong. [BW]

She laughed so hard her water broke—and she wasn't even pregnant. [JR>]

Say what you like about Facebook, it has totally revolutionized how we waste our lives. [AN]

It brought a tear to my eye—my glass eye. [RW]

Here, summer is always 9 months of anticipation—and 3 months of disappointment. [TG>]

I'm going to make a prediction about the game—it could go either way. [RA]

Money isn't everything—but it tends to keep the children in touch. [MA^]

Insanity is hereditary—you get it from your kids. [~EB]

Don't worry about old age—it doesn't last.

The human mind is the most remarkable of all creations. It starts working even before we are born, and works continuously 24 hours a day collecting and storing information, and never stops—until we stand up to give a speech at Toastmasters. <sup>HP^</sup>

The guy who invented the first wheel was an idiot. The guy who invented the next three—he was the genius. <sup>AN</sup>

I spun around and — wham! — I hit Sam Wilson's belt buckle right in the forehead. He was the assistant principal. As I lay on the floor looking up at Sam, who was as tall as a house, he leaned over and helped me up — by my right ear. <sup>RJH</sup>

Forget Louisville. Forget Nashville. The name of my town is Opinionville. <sup>SK^</sup>

I promise to tell the truth, the whole truth, and nothing but the truth—unless I think it adds to my story! <sup>RD^</sup>

The word "cereal" is from the Greek "ceres"—meaning "Free Toy Inside." <sup>CM</sup>

I have become a radical baby boomer. When I crossed the "50 line" last year, I looked around for something that was good about being 50 —I found absolutely nothing. <sup>WJ^</sup>

I was living the dream—until my first day in second grade <sup>TB^</sup>

Look at Evel Knievel: the man has made millions of dollars—for his team of orthopedic surgeons. [TC+]

Blessed are the young, for they will inherit the national debt. [HH]

I don't care what's written about me, so long as it isn't true. [DP]

I hate housework! You make the beds, you do the dishes—and 6 months later you have to start all over again. [JR]

I find television highly educational. Every time someone turns it on, I go into another room and read a book. [GM]

I offer my opponents a bargain—If they will stop telling lies about us, I will stop telling the truth about them. [AS]

In Oklahoma, we have an average annual rainfall of 31.2 inches, and boy, you ought to be there the day we get it. [WR]

Our town was so small we didn't have a town drunk—so we all took a turn.

My greatest nightmare was coming true. I already knew I wasn't good enough to be a lady, but now I wasn't even good enough to get a job. That night I asked my roommates for advice —"Mom, Dad …" JL^

My marriage is on the rocks again. Yeah, my wife just broke up with her boyfriend. RD

There is this guy who, every time I see him, says something wonderfully tactless like—"Oh, looking a little older since last time. Oh, nice sunglasses, they hide your crow's feet. Ah, you used to be so handsome." This idiot, this master of tact, is my worst enemy—and his name is—Mirror. ~ SJ^

There we were, three macho teenagers, Taylor, Eric and, well—two macho teenagers—and me. RA^

Remember you're unique—Just like everybody else. MM+

I decided to study in a state that is very dear to us Indians—Indiana. Where tall skyscrapers and great fashion—do not exist. ~SK^

College classes were a big buffet. Looking at me, you can see I loved going to class. [Speaker is a big man.] WM^

If you're 5 minutes early—you're already 10 minutes late. [VL]

The secret of life? — Have rich parents. [JW^]

I went to my Oxford interview. Three o'clock sharp. Three professors on the panel. Four glasses of sherry. [SB^]

If the phone doesn't ring, you know it's me [JB>]

My wife and I signed up for ballroom dancing—actually, my wife signed us up for ballroom dancing. [JG^]

People started to ask me: When are you going to get married and start having children? — [I replied] Why, is there a shortage? [JL^]

Things are going to get a lot worse before they get worse. [LT+]

To be rich, find out what poor people are doing—then don't do it! [MA^]

To be truly effective as a driving instructor you need patience, perseverance and—valium! [DW+]

Thrift is an admirable virtue—especially in your parents.

Today a man knocked on my door and asked for a small donation towards the local swimming pool—I donated a glass of water.

Tess was a one-man woman—with a short attention span. [MW]

We are in a battle between the Haves vs the Have Mores.

As kids, fun was drawing chalk marks on the pavement—around crumpled bodies.

We Southerners aren't fatter—we're just more honest.

When I got through with him, he was all covered wit' blood—my blood! [JD]

I can't die—I'm booked up for the next five years. [GB]

I cook with wine—sometimes I even add it to the food. [WCF]

Forecasting is difficult—especially about the future. [YB]

I didn't mind my mother-in-law living with us—but you'd think she could have waited until after we were married.

Walmart built a wedding chapel in one of its Las Vegas stores. The store's return line now extends out the door.

How many of you know that if you had your life to live over again, you'd do more? How many of you know people who are not living up to their full potential? And how many of you saw one of those people when you looked in the mirror this morning? [DP^]

I don't find it hard to meet expenses. They're everywhere.

I don't know about you, but my day begins at the crack of noon.

I asked a friend in the police force what he'd do if he had to arrest his own mother. He said "Call for backup!" [JM^]

I love shopping for shoes. It's the only place where a man tells me I'm a 10. [PD]

He's so clever sometimes he doesn't understand a single word of what he's saying. [~OW]

I squeezed four years of College into six.

If we're here to help others, what are the others here for? [GHP]

If you don't read newspapers you are uninformed; if you do read newspapers you are misinformed. [MT]

If you look like your passport photo, you probably need the trip.

If you look like your passport photo, you're too ill to travel. [JP]

Isn't it ironic that the colors red, white, and blue stand for freedom—until they're flashing behind you? [~FC]

Life is like math—full of problems. [RJ^]

My education was dismal—went to a series of schools for mentally disturbed teachers [WA]

My opinion might change—but not the fact that I'm right.

My wife thinks I'm cool. Well, she thinks I'm not so hot. [LC^]

Oh, the disappointment. He was supposed to be THE ONE. Why couldn't I find someone to love, the way Donkey loves Shrek, or the way Kanye West loves—Kanye West. [DB>]

One day, out of the blue, I learned that my wife was a great motivational speaker. She said: "You find a job or I'll quit mine." [JN^]

She got her good looks from her father—he's a plastic surgeon. [GM]

Some people quit looking for work as soon as they get a job.

We should always live within our income—even if we have to borrow to do so.

When I was a kid, all I knew was rejection. Even my yo-yo never came back! [RD]

The best way to keep children home is to make the home atmosphere pleasant—and let the air out of the tires. <sup>DP</sup>

When I was still living with my mom, I walked up to her one day, and I said the words that all parents dream about, "Mom, I'm moving out of the house." My mom said, "Yes!" I'm joking—She was WAY more excited than that! <sup>AB^</sup>

Our college football team was different: we didn't have a victory song—just a song of surrender!

A celebrity is a person who works hard all his life to become well known—then wears dark glasses to avoid being recognized. <sup>FA</sup>

A graduation ceremony is an event where the commencement speaker tells thousands of students dressed in identical caps and gowns that "individuality" is the key to success. <sup>RO</sup>

A successful man is one who makes more money than his wife can spend. A successful woman is one who can find such a man. <sup>LT</sup>

Ancestry.com pegged me. I am 93% Phoenician and 3% Irish—that's why I drink so much. <sup>MA</sup>

As I hurtled through space, one thought kept crossing my mind—every part of this rocket was supplied by the lowest bidder. [JG]

Give a man a fish and he will eat for a day. Teach him how to fish, and he will sit in a boat and drink beer all day.

He's been here a *l-o-n-g* time—long, long before the Dead Sea ever felt sick.

Her parents were social drinkers—who happened to be very social. [MW]

His proudest accomplishment as a young man was being selected as one of the 10 Best Looking Men in Ohio —by the Ohio Blind Association. [BH^]

I can explain this to you—but I can't understand it for you.

I had a salad for dinner last night. Mostly croutons and tomatoes. Really, just one big, round crouton covered with tomato sauce. And cheese. Okay, FINE, it was a pizza. I had a pizza.

I fish, therefore I lie.

I haven't smoked much since I quit. <sup>SH</sup>

When things get rough and my kid and I need to talk, we have a special quiet place to sit down and talk—Dairy Queen. <sup>~RW</sup>

My wife received great advice on the birth of our child. *Being a mother is a blessing—just know that the first 40 years are the hardest.* <sup>~MW</sup>

If I had a dollar for every girl that found me unattractive, they'd eventually find me attractive. <sup>FC</sup>

I've been in love with the same woman for 27 years—if my wife ever finds out, she'll kill me!

I was 24 years old living in India. I had a nice job, nice car, and nice —— hair. [speaker was now bald] <sup>MV^</sup>

I never drink water because of the disgusting things fish do in it. <sup>WCF</sup>

I know my golf game is improving—I am hitting fewer spectators. <sup>~ GF</sup>

I lost my job due to illness and fatigue—my boss got sick and tired of me.

I was born a long, long time ago. In fact, it was a year before my first birthday.

I was going to give him a nasty look, but he already had one. ᵀˢ

I was trying to daydream but my mind kept wandering. ˢᵂ

I went to Harvard—the Clemson of the North.

I've had a lot of amazing luck over the past year—all of it bad!

If it wasn't for bad luck, I'd have no luck at all.

If at first you don't succeed, you're about average.

If I agreed with you, we'd both be wrong. ~ᴿᴸ

If you think nobody cares about you, try missing a couple of monthly payments.

Insurance has sure become expensive. They've overlooking that all I want is a policy—not the company.

IRS Motto: We've got what it takes to take what you've got.

Last month our preacher said there were 87 kinds of sin. The following week, requests for the list were overwhelming. ~RZB

My people skills are well above average. My tolerance for idiots needs some work.

The Detroit String Quartet played Brahms last night. Brahms lost. BC

No, I'm not crazy—I've just been in a terribly bad mood for 20 years.

Practice safe lunch—use a condiment.

Santa Claus has the right idea—visit people only once a year! VB

Southern women are more beautiful—the weather gives them more time to bloom.

Some ideas and opinions are so foolish you have to belong to the intelligentsia to believe them. [GO]

The problem with being punctual is that no one's there to appreciate it.

The world is getting so complex even teenagers don't have a simple solution.

There can't be a crisis next week. My schedule is already full. [HK]

There's only one thing in the world worse than being talked about—and that's not being talked about. [OW]

To drink, or not to drink?—What a stupid question!

*Veni, Vedi, Visa*: I came, I saw, I did a little shopping.

We are promised that the poor will inherit the earth—but without the oil rights. [HR]

We sleep in separate rooms; we have dinner apart; we take separate vacations. We're doing everything we can to keep our marriage together. [RD]

A politician is a fellow who will lay down your life for his country [TG]

Be nice to your kids. They choose your nursing home.

Don't worry about what people think. They don't do it very often.

Holidays have been ruined when children choke on pieces of plastic toys, get burned by a fireplace, or find Grandma's handgun. [GN]

Everybody's got to believe in something. I believe I'll have another beer. [WCF]

Everything is changing. People are taking comedians seriously and treating their politicians like a joke. ~[WR]

I admit that the Aussies have one important advantage over we Kiwis; they have the world's best neighbors.

God created the 10 Commandments—man created a billion laws to say the same thing.

I don't have a beer gut—I have a protective covering for my rock-hard abs. <sup>BM+</sup>

I am not afraid of dying. I just don't want to be there when it happens. <sup>WA</sup>

Yes, I have opinions of my own—really strong opinions—but I don't always agree with them. <sup>GHB</sup>

I knew Momma was looking for something to whip me with—Belt? Shoe? Chain Saw? <sup>JD^</sup>

Eat right. Exercise. Die like everyone else. <sup>MW</sup>

I met my wife on a cruise. Surprised me. I thought she was home in South Carolina.

Go, and never darken my towels again. <sup>GM</sup>

I thought I wanted a career. Turns out I really wanted a paycheck.

I took an IQ test—my results were negative. [TS]

I've been wrong only once, and that's when I thought I was wrong.

I'm not a scientist—and I have the grades to prove it [LG]

I'm not trying to evaluate his performance—just trying to locate it.

If you need a title, be imaginative. I know an auto mechanic who is now a "vehicle maintenance engineer." He repairs my Toyota—and drives a Mercedes! [RF^]

Jimmy Buffett was right: If we weren't crazy already, we'd all go insane.

Kids in the backseat cause accidents. Accidents in the backseat cause kids.

Most pro athletes are bilingual: they speak English and profanity. [GH]

My fake plants died because I didn't pretend to water them. [MH]

My parents worked out that I wasn't a General Manager—I was just being generally managed. [KYY]

My wife has a slight speech impediment. Every now and then she stops to breathe. [JD]

The operation was a success—despite the patient dying.

Nothing makes it easier to resist temptation than a good upbringing, rock-solid values—and some witnesses. [JL>]

There's only one thing money can't buy—poverty. You need a credit card to do that. [PW]

To err is human, to forgive—is highly unlikely.

We've been married for 15 great years—and 16 not-so-great years!

We've been married so long we're onto our 4th bottle of Tabasco!

What's the penalty for bigamy? Two mothers-in-law. [RBZ]

You should always go to other people's funerals—otherwise, they won't come to yours. [YB]

A friend is someone who will help you move. A TRUE friend is someone who will help you move a dead body.

A verbal agreement isn't worth the paper it's written on. [SG]

An interesting finding in a new Mayo Clinic Study is that Organics do, indeed, cause weight loss—of your wallet.

Don't worry. I don't have a license to kill—just a learner's permit.

Ever stop to think—and forget to start again?

Experience is something you don't get until just after you need it.

He's tough. If I ever needed a heart transplant I'd want his—it's never been used.

God loves stupid people. I know—He made SO many of us.

A new bank has opened in our town advertising "24 Hour Banking." But it didn't entice me to open an account—I don't have that much time.

I had a job I didn't like. I hadn't had a date in three years. And I had a couple of roommates named Mom and Dad. LM^

My conscience is clear—I don't use it.

My kid's college major is extracurricular activities.

My dad came up to me and said, "Son, it's okay. You've flunked your exams; you already got arrested. That's fine—you get that from your mother's side" DH^

Hadn't seen him for 20 years. Wouldn't have recognized him if it hadn't been for the suit.

In the late 90's, both neophytes and the greedy bought dotcoms with no earnings, no business plan and no clue.

Camping is when you spend a small fortune—to live like a homeless person. CG

I love children—I used to go to school with them. [HR]

Never underestimate your abilities. That's your boss's job.

Some dog I have. We call him Egypt—he leaves a pyramid in every room. [HR]

No man goes before his time—unless the boss leaves early. [GM]

Sometimes I wake up grumpy — sometimes I let him sleep.

Spend more time with a real book—not Facebook.

The only people we think of as normal are those we don't know very well. [SF]

He always brightens up a whole room—every time he leaves.

There are two days in the week I never worry about—yesterday and tomorrow [RB]

This is your captain speaking: "Please fasten your seatbelt. Be sure your seat is in the upright position. We are about to take off." Don't you just love this sound?—I hate it! [MQ^]

A fellow who thinks he's a wit is usually half right.

A fool and his money are soon elected. [WR]

A fool and his money can throw one heck of a party.

A journey of a thousand miles starts with a single cash advance.

Behind every Prince Charming is a castle to be cleaned.

Blessed are the young—they shall inherit our mess.

He's hard to dislike—until you really get to know him.

I'm not sure about him. Is he onto something—or is he on something?

Real men don't ask for directions—that's why some guy invented GPS.

Sobering, isn't it? Half the people we know are below average.

We live in a new era where our check is good but the bank might bounce.

When young, I wanted girls to be running after me—so I became a bus driver.

When young she was such a knockout she stopped the traffic—and made it go backwards.

Wise men speak because they have something to say; fools speak because they have to say something. [P]

Women sometimes make fools of men—but most guys are the do-it-yourself type.

Always borrow money from pessimists—they don't expect it back.

Brains are wonderful. I wish everyone had one.

X-Rated movies are all alike—the only thing they leave to the imagination is the plot. <sup>TS</sup>

My boss just completed writing a book. He got the title right: *I came, I saw, I exploded.*

Tennis is an amazing sport—it's where unseeded players can still flower.

Hard work has a future payoff. Laziness pays off now. <sup>SW</sup>

At every party, there are two kinds of people: those who want to go home and those who don't—and they're usually married to each other. <sup>TW</sup>

Don't steal—that's the government's job.

My wife wins most arguments—her mother wins the rest. <sup>HY</sup>

What do you call an intelligent, good-looking, sensitive man? — A rumor.

I married my wife for her looks—but not the kind I now get. <sup>~HY</sup>

Decision-making in our house is simple: I just say, "Honey, we are NOT going and that's—semifinal."

My mother was determined I would learn to ride that bike even if it killed—me. ᴰᴺ^

My first boss rarely smiled so I've never forgotten the first time I made him laugh—I asked for a raise.

My wife ran off with my best friend last week—I miss him! ⱽˢ

Losing a husband can be hard—in my case, it was almost impossible. ᵀᵂ

Men never get lost—they simply find themselves in unexpected places. ᴷᴷ^

The reason for elections is obvious—to see if the polls were right.

We have the best politicians in the world—the very best money can buy. ~ᵂᴿ

Don't vote—it will only encourage them.

Our country desperately needs more unemployment—of politicians.

I woke up in the hospital with some memory loss. Doctors examined my brain; they found nothing — nothing wrong with my memory. [JA^]

Your speech draft is both good and original; but the part that is good is not original, and the part that is original is not good. [~SJ]

You can tell I am ethically flexible. [~JA>]

I installed a skylight in my apartment. The people who live above me are furious! [SW]

No matter how busy a man is, he is never too busy to stop and talk about how busy he is.

I love the motto of the Cremation Society—*Think outside the box!*

I'm not old—just chronologically gifted!

When given a choice between two evils, choose the one you've never tried. [~MW+]

# Asides

An Aside is a brief humorous conversational comment, usually in the form of an insider's explanation, elaboration, or observation. Typically, it is delivered after a pause, in a different tone or octave, and accompanied by appropriate facial expressions.

Imagine being in the audience listening to this speaker:

*At 8, I finally rode my bike. To celebrate, my mother and I took the training wheels off— (now) don't get excited, we only took them off the front wheel.* <sup>DN^</sup>

The first part is the situation; the second is the insider's comment. We can readily picture David Nottage, the 1996 World Champion Speaker, leaning into the audience with a conspiratorial, impish tone and expression, telling us, "Don't get excited."

David soon followed with another insider's laughter-generating comment:

*Mother had a bright idea—Oh, this one was a gem!*

Compared with the short punch line of Twists, Asides are more conversational and explanatory. Twists are placed only at the end of sentences; Asides almost anywhere.

An example of an Aside inside a sentence comes from a speech by Linus Chang:

*And we used the GPS satellite navigation device instead of a map ... I was happy because I could listen to Jane, the voice inside the GPS. With her smooth, sophisticated and—let's face it, sexy—voice, Jane could tell me where to go, all-day and all-night long.*

In another speech, Linus gave us a double Aside:

*I kept my good looks—well, most of them—well, that's what my mother said.*

Like Twists, Asides are simple to create and bring smiles and laughter. And they bring something more: audience connection and attention. Asides are a more intimate form of conversation, with the audience feeling they are being given an insider's viewpoint. Further, each Aside is usually a statement addressed to each audience member, creating the desired effect of keeping them engaged with the speaker.

It should be no surprise, then, that Storytellers and speakers with a storytelling flair have Asides as an important part of their communication quiver. And as we are, at heart, all storytellers, we should have them as an active part of our communication quiver too.

## Lessons from Kelly Swanson

**Kelly Swanson** (http://motivationalspeakerkellyswanson.com) has developed a strong following in the business community where her examples of connecting and engaging through storytelling resonates. With Kelly's permission, I share some the many Asides that have kept her business and non-business audiences engaged—and laughing—and returning for more. The Asides come from a wide variety of the stories she tells, and demonstrate the connective mind of a great storyteller.

*I'm a speaker, which means I love the lights, I love the stage—and I'm one bounced check away from living out of my car.*

*I speak at a lot of women's health events—I'll pause while you gasp in shock—*

*After my presentation —Yes, it went well, thanks for asking! — I rushed to…*

*I was tucking my young son into bed. We'd been through the usual drill: bed-time story, glass of water, bathroom trip, monster check—and a rambling prayer that would have made Moses proud.*

*Mr Bean even had a sign made to tell everybody all the things that were—and weren't—in this healthy cake. It was quite a large sign—as most of the ingredients had more than three syllables— [Double Aside]*

*Mr. Bean smiled at the crowd of new friends. "Are you enjoying the cupcakes?" Everyone nodded and smiled—well, except for Erma, but they blamed her stiff expression on the Botox.*

*The reason I went from zero to six figures in a year—okay, 10 years—was …*

*The church had a long history in the community—I think Moses was a charter member—*

*The committee was more than willing to make changes—as long as we kept things the way they were for 100 years.*

*They were embarrassed—I was carrying a copy of 50 Shades of Grey.*

If interested in the pausing and gestures that accompany these and many other lines, YouTube has a variety of Kelly's presentations listed under Kelly Swanson Speaker.

## Comment

As I re-read Kelly's Asides, my mind recounts the scenes: Kelly's facial and other gestures when delivering them, the laughter that followed, and the enjoyment of being in her audience, experiencing her presentation.

Now that you know the simple recipe, it's time to start building your own personal humor chest of Asides.

# Asides ~ Examples

I like to sit and think—well, mainly sit.

For people in society with too much time on their hands—which obviously includes you —why else would you be here? ~CM

As my dad got older, his hair kept receding. One day he returned from the barber, triumphant. No longer was he charged for his haircut—but his barber now wanted to charge him a search fee.

My two girls were adopted. My two boys, however, I birthed the hard way—with a lot of screaming and tears—and that was just from my husband! SL^

Everything I learned was at my mother's knee—and other low joints. AS

I have a degree in Liberal Arts—would you like fries with that?

Our meeting facilities today would generously be called frugal—for any English major among us, that is spelt CHEAP. ~JR>

I was lost in thought—it wasn't familiar territory. ~TS

After 4 years of Business School I went for the American dream. I bought a Subway sandwich shop—you're all impressed—I can tell. DLC

He was a decent man—despite an intellect somewhere this side of Einstein.

Do you know what is wrong with the world? Do you know what is wrong with me? Do you know what is wrong with you? — WHO CARES!!??? — The question is, what is right with the world? LM^

I believe in practicing prudence—well, at least once every two or three years. ~MI

I once met Wayne Newton in Las Vegas. We were playing Black Jack together—well, he was at the $1,000 table—I was at the $5 table. But we were rubbing shoulders— well, he was 35 feet away—but he looked at me—once—I think. ~CW+

I became consumed by this dilemma and desperate for an answer. I turned to books, coaches, meditation—you name it, I did it!—I even searched in the bottom of a bottle of whiskey—I eventually found my answer. MH^

I spent 14 years at school—most of it in the corridor.

I was a teenager and my parents were desperate—sounds familiar, doesn't it? [VJ^]

Even today, we are judged by the color of our hair—well, some of us! [Speaker bald] [RD^]

I'm five foot four—when I'm really trying. [LSR]

My 9-year old brother was poised on the 12-foot high diving board. He didn't swim. Hadn't seen water except for a bathtub—and we couldn't get him in that. [EP^]

One day a co-worker and I did a technical presentation of congested highway intersections. My co-worker did most of the talking—he's not a Toastmaster. [JA^]

Been there, done that—got the T-shirt! [JE^]

We were all playing around in the water. The kids were being high maintenance, of course — as were their fathers! [RR^]

*I did it my way* (singing)—I never said I was singing well. [CV^]

I don't want to brag but I took a $60,000 debt and in six short months I doubled that debt—I turned my Subway sandwich shop into a non-profit organization. [DLC]

After successfully completing college, I found a great girl — but not a job. [DH^]

Apathy is becoming a major problem — but who cares?

My children are all tall and thin—they eat like longshoremen—and a couple swear like sailors, too. [~SL^]

First things first—but not necessarily in that order.

Think of your journey. Do you know where you are right now? — Do you really care? [KK^]

Guys have feelings too—but then, who cares?

"There you go Mr Tate. Next time, drive a little slower." — Speaking of slow, have you ever wondered why it takes a police officer so long to write a ticket? [ET^]

As I took note of the perfectly rounded weight, I could only say "Wow"—Backwards, that's "WOW!"—I mean I was so impressed … ᴱᴴ^

Full name is Bobby Backwards, Bob for short—because Bob backwards is … well. ᴿᴹᴷ

CRACK!! (Tree limb breaks.) A-h-h-h (Slowly begins to fall)—Have you ever noticed that life-changing events always seem to happen in slow motion? ᴰᵂ>

Gentlemen, those are my principles—and if you don't like them, I can change them. ᶜᴮᴰ

He's a crazy nut case—that's a technical term. ᵀᶜ>

He's a great guy—once you get through his titanium exterior.

I always like to do that—just to see your faces!

Several years later—I'm a slow learner—I realized that…

I hit a swarm of bugs. There were thousands of them! — Well, there were hundreds of them—okay, there was one of them—but it was a BIG one. [DW>]

I can never forget this incident for two reasons: my wife won't let me forget it— it has too much entertainment value for her—and because of how I felt that evening [VJ^]

Next month I turn 50. Only this morning I was thinking there is no way I can really be that old—as I took my blood pressure medicine! [LL^]

I was about to tell Joanna my plans when the Universe changed them: my blood sugar dropped dramatically. When your brain springs into corrective action, you lose emotional control and rational thought—you know, those are a couple of things you don't need on a first date! [LL^]

She notices I'm starting to look a little goofy—okay, goofier than usual. [LL^]

I was relaxing on the couch, watching the New York Knicks beat the Orlando Magic, when my very pregnant wife says, "We need to talk"—which means she'll do all the talking—"To help us with the new baby, my mother has agreed to move in with us." [ML^]

It's dark. I'm in a barn with no electric power. There's a cow strapped to a post with a rope. And back here is a cold cowboy aiming his flashlight, poorly—Would you like to talk about a bad day at the office? [MM^]

Lawyers have feelings too—allegedly.

Mama held my head in her arms until I stopped sobbing—and the neighbor's dogs stopped howling <sup>RJH</sup>

The boy's mother was a nurse in the ICU—which, by the way, never made much sense to him—every time somebody asked about it, he said, *I see you too*—but I'm digressing. <sup>DH+</sup>

I have 4 principles—aptly named 1 to 4. <sup>JY^</sup>

I read the paper occasionally—depends when my neighbor is away. <sup>BM^</sup>

I looked at all those people judging me—like you guys! <sup>JN^</sup>

Then I remembered the words of my high school football coach. "Men" —all right, you caught me, he didn't call us men—"Ladies." <sup>JW^</sup>

When I quit my bartender's job, I went on tour with a stripper for the summer. I wrote home weekly—to lessen parental concerns—giving them a comic exposé of exposeurs. <sup>RS^</sup>

Australians are descended from a long line of tall, bronzed warriors and athletes—and they're still descending. [JE^]

He's a relation of mine—through drink. [HR]

Heaven knows that I cannot wait to get off this stage and get some clothes back on—and that's a sentence I never thought I'd have to say. [KH^]

I became a wannabe entrepreneur. This man offered me buckets of money to build him a website—new car, here I come! [RA^]

I like to move around the stage when speaking—it's harder to hit a moving target.

I love my wife—you know I'm related to her by marriage? [HR]

I was evaluating others—using the Sandwich Method, of course. [WP^]

I was trying to get an engineering-type to understand me. It was bad—it was like getting an accountant to understand—no, that's not true—they are worse!

Whatever the critics may think—which is something I seriously doubt. [JE]

I went jogging last week—hadn't planned to—but it was a scary neighborhood.

Incomes are falling—as I'm sure you've noticed.

It was 2001, Houston Texas, and I—having noticed the number of girls showing interest in me bowed to tradition—yes friends, I was going to have an arranged marriage. [VJ]

It was 2008 and the world economy had bottomed out—and so had I. [KK]

It was a perfect summer day. The temperature was 70 degrees. The humidity was low and there was a slight breeze—that blew through my hair [speaker bald]. [JW]

It happened—to my complete non-surprise.

It was as if my reflection stepped out of the mirror and walked over to me and looked me in the eye and stared me in the face—I told you I had a lot of conversations with myself. [CV]

Now under a public disclosure agreement I'm not allowed to say the name of the company that bought out my company [leaning into audience as if whispering a secret], but the company's initials are IBM. <sup>RH=</sup>

Oh, I would have traded my syringe for a bottle of champagne—except the foal was such a sloppy drinker. <sup>~MM^</sup>

One evening I hear this huge crash and then—something worse—silence! I come careening down the stairs to see my youngest son lying on the floor amongst a slew of decapitated Greek gods—funny sentence, not a funny scene. <sup>KH^</sup>

So mom and I went back to the Swami. "Ask yourself question. Who are you?"—Have you ever looked at modern art and wondered which side is up? <sup>VJ^</sup>

The car was swerving this way and that—it's a good thing I missed the bridge abutment! <sup>RHJ</sup>

Then I got hooked on meditation—did you know meditation was cool? <sup>VJ^</sup>

The other weekend I went to the lake with some of my girlfriends, and their husbands, and their kids. Me? I was the only one there without a boyfriend. BUT, I looked the best in a bathing suit—kids make your boobs sag, apparently!!! <sup>RR^</sup>

They won't discriminate against you because of your grey hair—or lack of it—you grey panthers and bald eagles. [RF^]

We both grew up in small towns. Jay's hometown was larger. It actually had a traffic light. My hometown didn't need one—we didn't have an intersection. [BM^]

There I was on the couch watching TV—trying my hardest not to think of anything else.

We're told that the average person has 40,000 thoughts a day—I hope not—for here it is, 2PM, and I've had only 10. [JN^]

You can set any destination you want on my GPS, even choosing the shortest or the fastest route—or, if you have kids, the Fast Food route. [LC^]

At least one good thing came out of that family reunion: she'd never ask me to swim again—probably for fear I'd say yes. [CW+]

Fat Dad loved my Mama. When they walked in the garden or sat on the sofa their hands seemed to find each other. When Mama watched TV, Fat Dad would wrap his arms around her and rest his chin on her shoulder, kiss her on the cheek—— Ooh!!! I couldn't believe old people carried on like that!!!! [RJH]

Attitude is everything. It determines success or failure. Mae West lived into her eighties believing she was twenty—it never occurred to her that her arithmetic was lousy. [AN]

Have you ever seen a sausage in its casing? — Have you ever been a sausage in its casing? [CW+]

I did a swan dive that would have won an Olympic gold medal—if there had been a category for "motorcycle ejects rider." [DW>]

I joined the East Meets West Club—not to be confused with the West Meets East Club.

I'm not tense—just terribly, terribly alert.

My teachers were telling my parents—at a "specially convened-meeting" of the PTA. [BR^]

I kind of said: "Thank you for sharing that with me"—although my mind was thinking of something QUITE different!

I regret this action now, as it led some of my friends astray—but then, on second thought, maybe I don't. [~CM]

I went home to see Dumb and Dumber. These guys were constantly bringing people back to our apartment. It was driving me nuts! But I went in and I said, "You make friends faster than anyone I know, and that is a gift." To see their faces—I swear they got smarter right before my eyes! LM^

Let me tell the Democrats, let me tell the mainstream media—although I repeat myself. TC>

My momma wasn't laughing though. When I got home that night, she treated me to the hickory stick waltz. You know what I mean—a piece of kindling from the wood box applied to the backside in steady rhythm. RJH

My motorcycle hit the trees, they were slapping my face—well, at least they cleaned the bugs off my goggles! ~DW>

Let me ask you a question that may seem a little strange. How many of you chose your parents? How about your kids?—I bet some of you wish you had! ~VJ^

My wife has a job. She goes to the salon on Saturdays — to make lots of church hair for Sunday—you can tell we live in the South. MA

So, here I am at the tender age of 29 and beginning my second MAJOR mid-life crisis!!!!!! I had my first when I was 24—but this one is much, much worse! RR^

Ssshhh, we can fix the fence. I'll buy another fountain. We can even replace that old car. Those are just things, but I could never replace you—besides, the town will be talking about this for weeks!!! RJH

The Blues deals with the hardship and sadness of life. With subjects like the dog died, the man cheated, the heart is broken, lost my job, can't pay the rent, woman left me, took the kids—AND the pink Cadillac—with the diamond in the back. DS^.

The ideal committee is one with me as chairman—and two other members who are in bed with the flu. AM

The Man of La Mancha dared to dream the impossible dream. While I dare not sing that song—for fear it could be your nightmare—I—like many of us here—have dreamed impossible dreams. ~MH^ [Double Aside]

There are millions of people out there who can't afford a single pair of shoes. Many of us have 20 pairs—ladies 50 pairs. PS^

There's a commercial on television which shows a gentleman walking through the front door and saying to his wife, "Honey, I'm home—forever!" RF^

The Swami showed me that the answer is not in that magic pill—or with Dr Phil!—the answer is always inside. VJ^

I settled in this country, found an engineering job, became a father, and got married—not exactly in that order. ᴶᴬ^

He was full of unsolicited advice—something he termed great suggestions.

I rejoined Toastmasters—despite its strange rituals. ᴸᶜ^

I see your faces—I can tell what you're thinking—Jay, get a life! ᴶᴺ^

Life is a moderately good play—although the third act needs lots of improvement. ~ᵀᶜ

Middle age is when you choose your cereal for the fiber—not the toy. ᶜᴹ

I love being over 70. I learn something new every day—and forget five others.

The younger generation—I'm talking about those who don't remember a world without Amazon, iTunes or Google—

Adult education has been around forever—it's called marriage.

She wasn't the kingdom's prettiest little girl, nor could she run the fastest, hold her breath the longest, or—though she might have bragged otherwise—eat the most pies at the county fair. [DB]

So I asked (my reflection) the next obvious question. I looked at him and said "Reflection"—because that's what I call him—"how do I stop myself from spinning away from my spirit?" [CV^]

I turned to my two sons, and said: "Guys, what did you learn from this?" My 16-year old said ... "I learned that my dad cries at the movies." My 12-year old took the question—and his wellbeing—a bit more seriously. He replied ... [JK^]

I've been working at home for the past few weeks. Never realized how much my wife buys from Amazon. There's a delivery every day. Well, that's not completely true. Some days there are two deliveries. [AW]

These beach babe spotting reports are accompanied by editorial comments—usually delivered in words of one syllable—or less. [JE^]

It's like 120 degrees in the shade—but there is no shade. The good thing is that there's a woman behind every tree—but there are no trees. [AN]

... Even if he told the truth I wouldn't believe him ...

# Putdowns

Putdowns are statements where the speaker humorously or lightheartedly belittles or otherwise makes fun of himself or herself. Such as:

*Don't be concerned—my electrons just aren't flying in formation today.*

*Forgive my appearance. I always look disheveled—my suits are custom-wrinkled.*

*My brain is like the Bermuda Triangle—information goes in, gets lost, and is never found again.*

*I have a Masters in Economics. I chose that field because it's the only profession where you can achieve eminence without ever being right.*

Putdowns make people smile and laugh. Your self-deprecating words take you off your pedestal and show that you are a regular person comfortable at poking fun at yourself. As a result, audiences warm to you, creating a stronger connection and triggering greater receptivity to your message.

Roasts are the opposite of Putdowns. Their objective is, in good humor, to put down someone else. A scan of the Speaking section in any major bookstore will typically show many books on Roasts, yet none on Putdowns. So where do you find ideas for Putdowns? Easy—in a book on Roasts. Find roasts that make you laugh—then, if appropriate, convert them to Putdowns by personalizing them.

For example:

Roast: *Sam doesn't suffer from excessive humility.*

Putdown: *Forgive me, but I don't suffer from excessive humility.*

Roast: *Unfortunately, Sam never drank from the fountain of knowledge. Just gargled.*

Putdown: *Some people have drunk from the fountain of knowledge. Me? I only gargled.*

Many of the Putdowns in the examples that follow were once Roasts. Others were speakers' comments jotted down at meetings—but may have been Roasts before that. Putdowns work particularly well whether you are giving a speech or are a conference or contest chairman.

Putdowns also go beyond a few one-liners. A self-deprecating style can readily permeate a whole speech which acts as a strong bond-builder between you and your audience.

## Lessons from Darren LaCroix

Darren LaCroix (www.darrenlacroix.com) delivered one of the most memorable speeches in the history of Toastmasters International Speech Contests. It had a simple title, self-deprecating humor, a meaningful message, and an unexpected, unforgettable action—he fell flat on his face on stage! Twice! That day in 2001 he deservedly won the title of World Champion of Public Speaking®.

To view Darren's outstanding message-driven, humorous speech, with his unique and supportive facial gestures, visit: https://www.youtube.com/watch?v=puSUnj3gf_Y

His speech, *Ouch*!, which follows, is shared with you because it demonstrates how a Putdown theme can create laughter, bond the speaker to the audience, and help make the audience open up to its message. Darren's Putdowns are not so much one-liners (as are many of the examples in this chapter) but are of a broader, self-deprecating nature, sometimes a paragraph long. They are not excessive but judiciously sprinkled throughout the speech, an ideal model for Putdowns. The intent of its inclusion is to broaden your range of Putdown possibilities once you are comfortable with the basic one-liners.

*Ouch!* amusingly recounts some of Darren's hurtful failures and ends with an encouraging, memorable idea: *If you fall on your face, at least you are falling forward—you're making progress.*

Darren has kindly permitted its reproduction to show Putdowns in the context of an actual speech. As you read it, you will identify the variety of Putdown lines Darren used that both underpinned his speech and endeared him to the audience. To show how effective they were in context, included is my personal laughter volume rating each time laughter was triggered. The Putdowns were particularly popular.

Some of the more notable Putdowns that Darren used were:

*After four years of Business School I went out and went for the American dream. I bought a Subway sandwich shop—you're all impressed I can tell. I don't want to brag or anything, but in six short months I took a $60,000 debt—and I doubled that debt. That's right, I turned my Subway sandwich shop into a non-profit organization*

*I remember my ridiculous idea ... I'd be a comedian! But you have to understand my background—I wasn't funny. I wasn't considered a class clown. In fact, the first time my brother ever laughed at me was when I told him I wanted to be a comedian. Ouch!*

*Imagine my parents' reaction ... after seeing me fall on my face. And then I come home. (Hands in pockets). Mom ... Dad ... I want to be a comedian—I was met by silence...*

*After a year of struggling in the comedy world I'll never forget one night. I was bombing for 20 minutes—it was horrible.*

# Ouch! ~ Darren LaCroix ~ WCPS 2001

Laughter Levels (see superscripts):      Light [L1]      Healthy [L3]      Loud & Long [L5]

Can you remember a moment
When a brilliant idea flashed into your head?
It was perfect for you.
And then all of a sudden—
From the depths of your brain another thought
Started forcing its way forward through the enthusiasm
Until finally it shouted
"YEAH—great idea—but what if you— [L1]
[Falls on face on stage]  Fall—on your face?" [L1]
What do you do when you fall on your face?
Do you try to jump right up and hope no one noticed? [L3]
Are you more concerned with what other people will think—
Than what you can learn from this? [L1]
[Speaker still lying face down on stage while speaking]
Mr. Contest Chair [L3] —Friends—
And the people way in the back! [L2]
 [Stands up]      OUCH! [L2]
Do you feel I stayed down too long? [L3]
Have YOU ever — stayed down — too long? [L1]

After four years of Business School
I went out and went for the American dream.
I bought—a Subway sandwich shop. [L2]
Oh yeah! [L1] — You're all impressed I can tell. [L1]
I don't want to brag or anything
But in six short months—I took a $60,000 debt—
And I doubled that debt. [L4]
That's right! — I turned my Subway sandwich shop
Into a non-profit organization! [L5]
I financially — fell on my face.

But then I remembered
I was not the only one
From my home town of Auburn
To fall on his face.

You see, 100 years earlier, my childhood hero, Dr. Robert Goddard
Had a ridiculous idea about building a device
To take off from the ground and reach the stars.
Dr Goddard was THE reason we landed on the moon.

I remember when I had my ridiculous idea.
I was listening to a tape of Brian Tracy—a great speaker.
He asked the question. He said:
"What would you dare to dream — if you KNEW you wouldn't fail?"
I struggled for an answer — and then — BING!!
I'd be a comedian! [L2]
But you have to understand my background —I wasn't funny. [L3]
I wasn't considered a class clown.
In fact, the first time my brother ever laughed at me
Was when I told him I wanted to be a comedian. [L3]
OUCH!! [L1]

Who do you want to be?
What changes do you want to make in your life?
So many of us can see clearly where we want to go.
And yet we go back and forth [Speaker paces back and forth]
If I just had more time—
If I just had a little more money—
If the kids were little older—
But we never take—that first step.

Dr. Goddard's first flight took off in Auburn—
And landed — in Auburn. [L3]
It only reached 41 feet — but it was a first step.

There are strangers out there—people who don't even know you—
Who will make fun of your first step.
When the local press found out about Dr Goddard's ridiculous idea
To reach the moon—and his first flight—
The next morning the headlines read
"Moon Rocket Misses Target by 238,799 and 1/2 Miles." [L2]
OUCH!! [L1]
But those strangers are part of your process.

We also have friends and family that love us
And don't want to see us fall on our face.
Imagine my parents' reaction
When after stretching their budget to help me through college
Seeing me fall on my face
And then I come home
[Standing with both hands in pockets]
"Mom—Dad — I want to be a comedian." L5
I was met by silence — (mouths a silent OUCH!) L2
They too are part of your process.

After a year of struggling in the comedy world
I'll never forget one night.
I was bombing for 20 minutes—it was horrible. L2
So I went for my sure-fire fix.
I brought a woman up from the audience.
And she stood directly behind me.
She put her hands forward in place of mine—
It's an old improv technique—
She would tell the story with her hand gestures
As I would tell it verbally.
And it works best the more animated the hands are.
Well this woman stood there like an ancient statue. L2
She didn't move — I turned to her in desperation and said—
"Just please do something with your hands." L1
She did — [Covers his mouth with his two hands] L4
OUCH!!!!!!!!! L1

I immediately called my mentor Rick.
I said: "Rick, I bombed! I died! They hated me!"
Rick said ... "SO??"
What do you mean "SO?"
How do you argue with "SO?" L2
And then Rick reminded me—
"Every comedian, every speaker
Anyone who has accomplished anything—
Has fallen on their face."
It's part of your process.

And then I remembered SUBWAY.
I fell on my face—but I never took the next step.
It's the step AFTER the Ouch that's so important —
It's so difficult.
We don't like the Ouch.
We don't want to take that step
But when that foot lands—
Oh, you're going like that feeling—
We learn from the Ouch.

In his effort to reach the moon Dr. Goddard said:
"Failures I consider valuable negative information—
Information essential to each step getting closer to the moon."
Dr Goddard was an Ouchmaster. [L2]
We need to be Ouchmasters.

If you are willing to fail — you can learn anything.
I still have my day job—
But now in my home town in a comedy club my picture hangs on the wall
Because I took the step after the Ouch!
I wasn't given the gift of making people laugh—
I was given the opportunity to take the next step.
So were you.
What's your next step?
When will you take it?
Take it!
I didn't want to look back on my life and think—
"Never did try that comedy thing — but instead I paid all my bills!" [L1]

We're all going to move forward and try and reach a point
But we're going to reach a point headed to our goals
Where we get stuck—and we can't move.
And if we're so afraid of that Ouch—we forget
That if we lean forward and take a risk
[Falls face down on floor again]
And fall on our face
[Stands up]      We still made progress. [L5]
Go ahead and fall!
Fall forward! [L5++]

# Putdowns ~ Examples

When I was born, the doctor came out to the waiting room and said to my father, "I'm very sorry. We did everything we could—but he pulled through." [RD]

Here I am — all ready to create dullness in the meeting!

Now don't believe what you see—there's a lot less to me than meets the eye. [~MM]

I'm not a failure. I started at the bottom and just happened to like it there. [JL>]

I'm a very mature thinker—all my ideas are at least 50 years old.

I'm so old, my daughter asked if my blood type has been discontinued.

I'm an opportunist—I never miss an opportunity to miss an opportunity.

I was a shy, scrawny kid—prime knuckle bait for the playground bullies.

My first boss was always so positive about everything. One day he said, *I just don't know how we could ever get along without you—but, beginning tomorrow, we're going to try.*

Understand that I'm the sort of guy who keeps talking until I say something.

On one occasion when I was lost, I saw a policeman and asked him to help me find my parents. I said, "Do you think we'll ever find them?" He said, "I don't know kid. There are so many places they can hide." [RD]

Now—try to imagine me with a personality.

I'm proud to be a man of many parts—unfortunately, it was a poor assembly job. [~JL>]

Please slow down—my IQ is that of a fruit fly's.

I never open my mouth without subtracting from the sum of human knowledge.

I'm beginning to think that my sole purpose in life is simply to serve as a warning to others.

My wife and I were happy for twenty years. Then we met. [RD]

I set low personal standards—which I consistently fail to achieve.

I've started writing another book —I've already got all the pages numbered!

You'll have to excuse my behavior—I've been myself lately.

I buy expensive suits. They just look cheap on me. [WB]

My claim to fame is that I put the "super" in superficial.

Here I am—the wrong person at the right time.

My last speech had as much impact as pouring a glass of water into the ocean.

I'm so uncoordinated I couldn't even follow a dog on a leash.

I hope you enjoyed my speech and, if you didn't, I hope you had a good nap. <sup>CW</sup>

You might have noticed I have an underdeveloped sense of modesty.

I haven't lost my mind. Half of it wandered off and the other half went to look for it.

Heck, I was so ugly as a kid my mother had to tie pork chops to my ears to get our dog to play with me. <sup>~YC</sup>

At school, I liked helping my classmates. For example, I graduated in that part of the class that helped make the top 90% look smart.

Don't be taken in by my rough exterior—inside, I am just as ugly.

Right now, I am as confused as a cow on AstroTurf.

After I die, I shall be remembered for my greatest contribution—organ donor.

I don't have an attitude problem. You have a perception problem. <sup>VS</sup>

I get my money the hard way—I have to ask my wife for it. ~DB+

I told my kids I never want to live in a vegetative state, being dependent on some machine and lots of fluids—so they unplugged my computer and threw out my wine. ~BML

I was a real nerd. Graduated from Harvard Business School with their famed MBO degree—a Masters in Boring Others.

If my memory gets any worse, I'll be able to plan my own surprise party.

Let me warn you in advance: I have a speech impediment—I speak too much.

I was an overnight success. Mind you, 30 years is a very long night.

I'm heavy into R&D—Resting and Dreaming.

I'm not fat—just easier to see.

Forgive me, but I don't suffer from excessive humility.

I live in a real egghead community—I'm the village idiot. ~DB+

As a kid, I wanted to be an actor. My parents suggested *One Flew Over the Cuckoo's Nest*.

Am I ambivalent? Well, yes and no.

Sometimes when I'm feeling lonely, I open the window, look up, smile, and wave for a satellite picture. ~SW

Ancestry.com told me my forebears were perfect fudge: mostly sweet—with a scattering of nuts.

I once received a standing ovation—of one! BH^

As a kid, our house was on the corner of No and Where.

At my age, I have enough wrinkles to hold an eight-day rain.

Chaos, panic and disorder!!!—Ah! My work here is now done.

Everything I say is true—and, if it isn't—it would be if it was!

First of all, my heritage—I'm part Irish. Part English. And part clown. ~CM

Funny, I don't remember being absent-minded.

How do I define a gourmet restaurant? Easy. It doesn't have a drive-through.

I am a gourmet cook. My favorite 7-course meal is a hot dog with a 6-pack on the side.

I am as predictable as a roulette wheel.

I am at that stage in life when I no longer have a need to beat my head against a wall just because it feels good when I stop.

I am ethically uninhibited.

I am known for my bullock speeches—a point here and a point there and a lot of bull in between.BH^

I am not so much a has-been—more like a definite won't-be.

I'm not overwhelming, not underwhelming—just plain-vanilla whelming.

I've had amnesia as long as I can remember. [TS]

I couldn't even get a job as a spell-checker in the M&M factory.

I do the work of three men: Larry, Curly, and Moe.

I don't ignore people—I just choose not to notice them. [TS]

I don't deserve this honor—but then, I have arthritis and I don't deserve that either. [JB]

I don't have an attitude. I just have a personality you can't handle. [~VS]

My brain power wouldn't even brown a crouton.

I don't know about you, but at my age I'm really happy my bathroom mirror steams up!

I don't seek much from life—I'd be content just with an unfair advantage.

I don't suffer from insanity. Frankly, I enjoy every minute of it. <sup>VS</sup>

I don't worry much about the cops. Heck, if they arrested me for being smart, they'd have to let me go for lack of evidence.

I dress like an unmade bed. ~HY

I exercise daily: I draw the water, take a bath, pull the plug, and then fight the current.

I give a lot of my money to sick and lame animals—I bet heavily at the track.

I graduated from the School of Hard Knocks—earned a Bachelor's degree in Bungles and a Masters in Mistakes.

I have a fantastic fan club—they have a great meeting each year—under an umbrella.

I had a hair-raising up-raising.

I grew up in a really remote area. Wow! When I say remote, I mean remote! I mean, our house was six whole blocks from the nearest McDonalds.

I'm a real geek. I had a terrible car accident coming out of the Holland Tunnel—my whole life passed before me—and I swear it was all in PowerPoint. [DMM]

I hate writing—but I love having written. [DP]

I have a photographic memory—unfortunately the lens cover is glued on. [DM+]

I have a rare medical problem. I sometimes suffer seizures—of common sense.

I have an instinctive attraction to the edge of the envelope.

I have been praised for being is a man who thinks twice—before saying nothing.

I have the same mindset as Santa—I like to visit people just once a year.

I have been so blessed, I am leaving both my brain and body to Science—Science Fiction!

I have that dreaded furniture disease—that's when your chest has fallen into your drawers!

I have the attention span of a lightning bolt. [~RR+]

I have the consistency of a roulette wheel.

I like falling behind—it gives me more time to catch up.

I live in my own LaLa land—a land way beyond truth, reality, and fantasy.

I love Nature—in spite of what it did to me. [BM]

I love to sing and I love to drink scotch—although most people would rather hear me drink scotch. [GB]

I can resist anything—but temptation. [OW]

I like beating the 5 o'clock rush—I leave work at noon!

I am annoyingly honest. [MW]

I married well. My wife has the face for TV. I have the one for radio.

I may be older—but I'm very immature. [JM>]

I may look stupid. That, of course, doesn't mean I'm not. [MM]

I may not be that funny, or athletic, or good looking, or smart, or talented—now, where I was going with this?

I never argue with my doctor—he has inside information on me.

I never got on well with my mother—she cussed me out a lot. Strangely enough, she never saw the irony in her calling me a son-of-a-bitch. [~JN>]

I spilled Spot Remover on my dog. Now he's gone. [SW]

I swore to my parents I'd graduate on time—no matter how long it took me.

I was a sickly teenager—suffered a lot from the common cold shoulder.

I started out with nothing—still have most of it.

I suffer from Conditionitis —I keep waiting for the right conditions before doing something!

I was born at an early age—it was the most exciting thing that happened to me that day.

I was so busy mopping up the water I didn't have time to turn off the tap.

I was born modest—but it wore off. ᴹᵀ

I thought my parents would invite me to live at home after college—their graduation gift of four suitcases suggested other plans.

I was so far behind on the track team I thought I was first.

I was such a pain as a kid—my parents wanted to make me the poster boy for birth control. ~HR

I was the kind of kid your parents told you not to play with. BR^

I was trying to daydream, but my mind kept wandering. SW

I work 50 hours a week to be this poor???!!!

I'm not crazy—it's just that I've just been in a really bad mood for 30 years.

I'd sing this for you, but I don't want to end our evening early.

I'm a cowboy at heart—it's why I'm always looking for a saloon.

I'm a decisive person—I'm well-known for my definite maybes.

I'm a diverse sort of guy—half artist, half athlete, half-wit.

I'm actually a humble person—I'm much greater than I think I am.

I'm an incredible cook. Next week I'm a guest on the new TV show, *That's Inedible!*

I was in Graduate School. I wanted a summer job. I wanted to change the world. Translation: I was tired, depressed, and broke.

I'm beginning to think I've been working with glue for too long.

I'm from South Carolina—too small to be a republic; too large to be an insane asylum.

I'm in the twilight of a below-average career.

Don't come near me—I'm mentally infectious—your IQ might drop 20 points!

I'm just one French fry short of a Happy Meal.

I'm often wrong but never in doubt.

I'm proud to be multilingual. I know 3 French words—*cul de sac.*

I'm so ditzy, I could hide my own Easter eggs and never find them.

Look, I'm such a bad cook, I daren't lick my own fingers.

I'm the boss which, as a brave friend reminded me is, spelt backwards, a double SOB.

I've so security conscious, I even write Confidential on the postcards I send.

Friends, if my IQ falls any further, you'll have to water me twice a day.

Look at me—a master of mistakes, a connoisseur of stupidity.

If prizes were offered to the world's worst letter writers, I'd take top prize!

My close friends are wonderfully honest. They tell me that what they love most about my conversations are my occasional flashes of silence.

I'm not dull—I just cause dullness in others.

My contribution is important. I'm the keeper of the potted plants.

My cooking's so bad my family says grace after we eat.

Life's just not fair. What Mother Nature gave me, Father Time has taken away. [EMM]

I'm pleased to see that my fan club is here today—thank you both for coming!

My first job, when I was 16, was at McDonald's—and my career has pretty much gone downhill since then. [SS^]

My great plans for life have, alas, been airbrushed from history.

My luck is so bad that if I bought a cemetery, people would stop dying.

There I was—all flash—and no cash.

My singing ability is legendary—but only in my mind.

My wife gave up shopping for antiques—when she realized she married one.

My wife has heard most my speeches. There's one in particular that she loves. It begins: *Honey, I'll clean up and do the dishes!*

My wife says I'm a model husband. I checked the dictionary to see what she meant—a small imitation of the real thing.

No, I'm not an Alpha male — just a beta test for one.

Our chairman and I were on a first-name basis: he called me Brian; I called him Sir.

Philosophically, I'm a minimalist. I do as little as possible.

Recently, I spoke to a group that turned out to be quite small. The organizer was extremely apologetic for inviting a man of my stature to speak to such a small group. He said that he'd tried really hard to get a speaker of lesser stature—but couldn't find one.

Look, I'm so contrary, if I fell in the river they'd look for me upstream. ~EMM

The good news tonight is that we have something in common. You don't know what I'm going to say—and I don't either—yet.

The secrecy of my job prevents me from knowing what I am doing.

There I was—after three successful failures...

There I was—caught carrying a copy of *50 Shades of Grey*.

Times have changed—10 years ago I knew more than my phone.

Friends, I want you to understand that William Shakespeare, Thomas Jefferson, and I all share a common characteristic—our brains no longer function.

Until I was thirteen, I thought my name was *Shut Up*. JN

What upsets me is that half the lies people tell about me aren't even true. YB

Money talks—of course, for me it's usually saying goodbye.

That was the point when my ego slunk out the bottom of my socks.

Where I grew up, you could walk five blocks in any direction and not leave the scene of the crime.

With age comes wisdom. Unfortunately, in my case, age came alone.

At my age, I can single-handedly disprove Darwin's Survival of the Fittest Theory. [EMM]

You know, I believe I'd enjoy getting out of bed a lot more if I only had to do it three times a week—this every day routine is overkill.

I was so ugly, my mama had to borrow a baby to take to church.

[Speech Ending] Friends, you have no idea how it feels to come to the end of another brilliantly written and impeccably delivered speech — unfortunately, neither do I.

# Exaggeration

As a child, you probably visited the circus and laughed (and laughed) at the antics of the clowns. Every exaggerated action triggered smiles and laughter—including when they exaggerated smallness—remember when a huge number of clowns clamored out of the tiny clown car? The same reaction can be captured when speaking with ludicrously exaggerated words and images, be they elephantine or gnat-sized, as this chapter will demonstrate.

After becoming aware of this tool, you'll start discovering that both the material and the opportunity for exaggeration is everywhere.

In speeches, most exaggerations are captured in short sentences, while others are tied together to create humorous vignettes. Both are successful. Both are in this chapter.

When speaking, exaggeration is an excellent tool to add color, richness, and laughter to your presentation. It is also a memorable way to help audiences visualize your point, particularly when it is accompanied with supporting facial and physical gestures.

So, start your own Exaggeration file by drawing on the diverse examples that follow:

*He's so big, it takes two dogs to bark at him.* [YC]

*He's so big, he makes me look like I just fell off a charm bracelet.* [JN^]

*He can compress the most words into the smallest idea of any man I know.* [AL]

*She is 14 months pregnant—and in imminent danger of giving birth to a football team.* [JE^]

*Grammie (at 100) is living for the moment. She is scraping e v e r y last bit of peanut butter out of that jar of life—and then licking the spoon!* [EF^]

*You can take all the sincerity in Hollywood, place it in the navel of a firefly and still have room enough for three caraway seeds and a producer's heart.* [FA]

*Without music you are not living, you merely exist. Like a bear cub without its mother, like a shark in shallow water, like the ex-Chief Accountant at Enron!* [DS^]

*I was in love: all of a sudden, my life began to play out like a movie—smoke began to fill the floor, a light from the window shined on his face, and choirs of angels began to sing ... [then later] ... I fell out of love—the clouds vaporized and the angels went silent.* [Repeated several times throughout speech to great effect] [DB>]

## Lessons from Randy Harvey

After becoming comfortable with creating and using amusing exaggerations (which are primarily similes and metaphors that we learned about years ago in school), our next challenge is to craft and thread a series of exaggerated ideas into a vignette. Accomplishing that will herald your arrival on Humor Peak.

**Randy J. Harvey** (www.randyjharvey.com) creates exaggeration vignettes of all sizes. One of my favorites comes from *Lessons from Fat Dad*, the speech which earned him the World Champion Speaker crown in 2004. Imagine the fun he had conjuring up this vignette:

*I was driving one sunny afternoon,*
 *Singing to Simon and Garfunkel on my eight track—*
*"Cecelia you're breaking my heart."* [singing the line]
*A humungous horsefly shot through the window, in my mouth, down my throat.*
*It came back up — lodged in my right nostril.*
*What would you do with a horsefly buzzing in your nose—*
*Taking bites the size of Texas?*
*I steered with my knees and tried to fire that bug out my nose.*
*The car swerved to the left—then catapulted right*
*Cut down the Morrison's fence — sailing across their yard —*
*Right at Mossburger's fountain —*
*Where Mary Poppins stood — holding her umbrella — pouring water from a can.*
*I hit that fountain so hard I launched her like sputnik —*
*Mary Poppins hovered briefly <pause>*
*THEN WENT DOWN FASTER THAN A SPOONFUL OF SUGAR! <pause>*
*The Morrison's and the Mossburgers were a bit excited.*
*Not Fat Dad — he rode in like the cavalry — made peace with the neighbors.*

And from another speech Randy shared for this book:

*Did I tell you we raised hogs?*
*I had to go pick up three feeder pigs at the auction.*
*Loaded them in the back of my station wagon.*
*I'm driving home—*
*Suddenly realized why it wasn't a good idea to put hogs in my back seat —*
*One made a deposit!*
*Another one of them — it was a rather amorous pig —*
*Kept doing something with my right ear.*
*And the third thought he was a dog — stuck his head out of the window*
*Said "hello" to a passing car—which drove off the road into seven feet of water!*

## Comment

The preceding shows that a mixture of imagination and exaggeration is a potent brew to create smiles and laughter. As you read this chapter, take the ideas you like, pour them into your Exaggeration machine, crank it up, and see what it creates. Have fun!

# Exaggerations ~ Examples

He was so poor his only pet was a tumbleweed.

It was so ugly it made a porta-john look like a palace!

It was raining so hard the animals started to pair up.

I was so sensitive as a kid, to avoid rejection I used to Trick or Treat via mail order. [EF^]

He viewed the world as a cow regards passing traffic—with large, uncomprehending eyes.

Ships are getting so big you can now board one in Florida and get off in Cuba.

She had enough baggage to fill an airport carousel.

I'm living so far beyond my income that it may almost be said we are living apart. [~EEC]

Their home is so big they have a large riding lawn mower— and, inside the house, they have a large riding vacuum cleaner.

His high energy made me feel like a snail on Valium. ~ PF

I live in a small South Carolina town. I don't know about your town—but if it has a McDonalds, I am impressed. WM^

Compliments from our boss are truly treasured — they arrive about as often as Halley's Comet!

She had the looks that would make a bishop kick a hole in a stain-glass window. ~RC

The couple were so thin they looked like the beginning of a barcode. DK^

He's so hot-tempered, when he's mad he bursts into flames. KCG

His life centers on the limitless multiplication of unnecessary necessities. ~ MT

I had a job as exciting as an Excel spreadsheet. [RH^]

Families are like house plants—in need of constant watering. [NQ]

He's a shiver looking for a spine to run up. [PK]

College tuition costs have become so high our kids' debts are as big as small nations.

His kind of client went home to the places where the stars seem to reach down each night to touch the anointed. [AN]

I went to a tough parochial school, Our Lady of Corporal Punishment. My first teacher was Sister Mary Brutus. Even Rottweilers were scared of her. [AN]

On many days, the dampness of the air pervades all life—envelopes seal themselves and postage stamps mate with one another as shamelessly as grasshoppers. [EBW]

I was perfectly content having a rock as a pet. I had easily trained him to sit and stay. I wanted to teach him to roll over so he would gather no moss. [JN^]

I was so short in high school I used to pose as a bowling trophy KM^

I woke up in a hospital with machines lurking over me like vultures — a doctor to my left, a nurse to my right — "What happened?" — "Well you just had an episode of sustained monomorphic ventricular tachycardia." — "Is that English? — "You had a heart attack." — "Oh." RMK

In 1934, my Gran was about 16 months pregnant with her third child. JE^

He was hit so hard he saw tomorrow today.

In our small town, you know you're one of us if your home has wheels and your car doesn't. ~ JF

It is hard to grow up in the shadow of Death Valley and not be baptized, by full immersion, in the fire of Clemson football. MR+

When I did something poorly, I got the full Harry Potter novel version—with the witch and broom included! LSR

Dr. Goddard's first flight took off in Auburn—and landed—in Auburn. It rose 41 feet. The next day's press headline: Moon rocket misses target by 238,799 and a half miles. ~DLC

He's so big, when he got on the scales they read "To be continued."

He's so ugly, flies won't land on him. [YC]

At age 16, Greg was 6 feet tall, and weighed 240 pounds — of what I can only presume to be biological insulation. [DT^]

It was so cold that his words froze as he spoke. I had to put them in a frying pan to see what he was saying.

It's so hot, hens are laying hard-boiled eggs. [YC]

Just like the Foo Foo Bird, he kept running round in ever-diminishing concentric circles until it finally disappeared up its own fundamental orifice. [~RH>]

My boss was 50 shades of crazy. [DW^]

All of a sudden I saw a row of mailboxes approaching me faster than a galactic meteor[DW+]

My flat mates made Dumb and Dumber look like Einstein and Oppenheimer. <sup>LM^</sup>

My hometown was so poor it finally had to close its zoo. The chicken died. <sup>JN^</sup>

He smelt so bad that when he approached the bathtub, the water receded.

Once my wife gets an idea in her head, it's almost impossible to change. It took me about 100 times to persuade her to marry me. <sup>~KCG</sup>

One afternoon, Mom and I traveled to the old part of the city of Calcutta—where the houses were so close that sunlight was a myth. <sup>~VJ^</sup>

Our first three months of Paramedic training? Learning to say cardiac defibrillator. <sup>TC+</sup>

Picture your audience naked—that's just one of 4,279 suggestions I received from the folks back home on how to improve this speech. <sup>DS></sup>

She was as inconspicuous as a tarantula on a piece of angel food cake. <sup>RC</sup>

Sing? I can't sing—I have a voice like a vulture <sup>CB^</sup>

That's the store where shirt prices look like area codes.

We arrived at their home during their Festival of Litter.

Their pooled emotions wouldn't fill a teaspoon. <sup>DP</sup>

His occasional flashes of silence made his company so delightful.

He's so optimistic he'd go after Moby Dick in a rowboat with tartar sauce in his pocket. <sup>VS</sup>

Anyone with an IQ greater than a pickle knows that...

Even a sleeping dog could see that one coming.

Those who know us, understand we are connoisseurs of madness and gourmets of absurdity. <sup>BB</sup>

The team's extreme behavior was so disgusting that my quiet, soft-spoken, mild-mannered father-in-law transformed into the Four Horsemen of the Apocalypse with Death and Hell following behind. [AP^]

That would be like the National Council of Bishops coming out with a statement urging wife-swapping. [AN]

That period at the end of the first sentence is perfect. It's outstanding—definitely keep it! The rest of the speech, however, needs some attention...

Times are getting so tough that Joe Six Pack is settling down as Joe One Pack and the fabled engagement rock is now just an engagement pebble.

Your compliments would have embarrassed a man of greater fiber; fortunately, they found eyes only too willing to read more. Thank you for the inaccurate accolades. [CM]

Central Bankers are flying down the road without a GPS, destinations uncertain.

Every dime of deficit spending was yielded up as if it were a foot of No Man's Land.

Everything I tell you today is true—except for the stuff I make up.

He chased after them like a Leprechaun searching for his pot of gold.

He approaches every subject with a closed mind and an open mouth.

He behaves like a one-man clown car.

He doesn't live within his income—he has enough trouble living within his credit limit.

He felt dumber than a trout biting on a rubber cricket.

He gave the whimper of a wimp.

He had an office the size of Rhode Island.

He had more friends than a jailhouse cat.

He had to stop driving his car for a while—the tires were getting dizzy.

He has a face upon which character remains to be written.

He has about as many money worries as Warren Buffet.

He had all the spontaneity of an alarm-clock buzzer.

He has an IQ less than room temperature.

He has never been known to use a word that might send a reader to the dictionary. [WF]

He has the consistency of a roulette wheel.

He is as about as smart as a wet cornflake.

He has more degrees than a thermometer.

He is doing for central banking what the Titanic did for ocean cruises.

He is the perfect example of that old dictum: *Mediocrity always sinks to the top.*

He just opens his mouth and lets the wind blow his tongue around.

He lives in such a private community, even the police have an unlisted number.

His outbursts were as frequent and natural as a cow's flatulence.

He looked like something the dog keeps under the porch.

He mounted his favorite horse and went off in full verbal gallop.

He reacted like a divining rod— bending in all directions.

He resisted every new idea as though it was a contagious disease.

He started his standard squid-like maneuver, throwing up enough black, cloudy, viscous material hoping we'd forget the question we asked.

He takes great intuitive leaps from unwarranted assumptions to foregone conclusions.

He turned a color Sherwin-Williams never believed possible.

He warmly crushed my hand.

He was all over the problem like kudzu.

He was as lost as a submarine without a periscope.

He was in his favorite cigar shop—an island of tranquility in a sea of virility. [AN]

He was like a cowboy in a department store—seeing so many things he didn't need.

He was off like a turtle.

He was one can short of a six-pack.

He was so embarrassed he shrunk to the size of a phone book comma.

He was so fat it was easier to go over him than around him.

He wasn't smart—but he was trainable.

He's as dull as a parking meter.

He's been here longer than Murphy's had a Law.

He's in his ever-present, pre-creased, crumpled suit.

She was so ugly, even the tide wouldn't take her out. [CY]

He's likely to shrivel into a rumor.

He's never had an unspoken thought.

He's nothing but a coward with a linguine-filled spine.

He's so smooth he could sell a muzzle to a dog.

He's so tall, if he fell he'd be halfway home. [YC]

He's so tough, he uses mace as a breath freshener.

He's such a smoochzer, he has more good lines than Shakespeare.

His argument was as shaky as a two-legged stool.

His bathroom is as big as Penn Station.

His face is an envelope with no address on it.

His family tree ain't got no branches. [YC]

His mouth was so big he could whisper into his own ear.

With his newly-coined pompous phrase, he cruised the corridors of his mind looking for an idea to attach it to.

His office is like a museum—plenty to admire, nothing to be touched.

His past disappeared down a memory hole.

He was busier than a one-eyed cat watching nine rat holes.

His planet-sized brain was always in the clouds.

His rhetoric and reality zoomed down different roads.

I grew up in a tiny tinpot town, a mere flyspeck on the map.

He was having difficulty training new morticians on how to look solemn at a $50,000 funeral.

I shivered so much my teeth were ivory jackhammers, just pounding in my head. [MM^]

I sing like a bullfrog with laryngitis. [~PH]

If a hummingbird had his brain, it would be flying upside down and backwards.

If he becomes even more laid back, we'll have to water him twice a week.

If he were an inch taller he'd be round. [YC]

It's as difficult as choosing your own parents.

It smelt like a yoghurt factory with faulty air conditioning.

It was a road whose sole purpose seemed to be to have you look at trees while you went from nowhere to nowhere.

It was as phony as a $3 bill.

It was as useless as a submarine with screen doors.

It was so cold the polar bears put on their overcoats.

It was so hot you could pull a baked potato right out of the ground. ~YC

It was so dry I saw a tree chasing a dog.

She's so old, she was a waitress at the Last Supper.

It's as old as Greek philosophy.

It's like trying to slice a banana with an electric fan.

It's smaller than a wart on an ant's armpit.

Larry is such a great Conference Emcee, I hope he's offered the job through 2099!!

Like a Methodist who had inherited a distillery, the new leader seemed embarrassed when asked of his predecessor's practices.

You don't need an appointment with the Genius Bar to have this one explained.

You know it's time to diet when you nod one chin and the other two second the motion.

Like Blanche Dubois [in *A Streetcar Named Desire*] America is all too dependent on the fiscal kindness of strangers. [JL]

The audience's faces were a forest of Gone Fishing signs.

My hometown was so small that the barbershop quartet had only three members.

My perspective was like that of racing through the Louvre on a motorbike.

My State is blessed with Senators Rock Solid and Mental Mush.

Like focusing on one eye in a Picasso portrait, it was only one of many features that seems to be out of place. [BB]

No surprise he changes his mind so often—his website is weathervane.com

Miss Mamo must have known that boy was coming because as soon as she saw him her eyes got really big like it was Christmas and she said, "Oooh, sweet Baby Jesus." [DH+]

Our Government suffers from fiscal incontinence.

The task was as difficult as identifying our dumbest Congressman.

Parliament rode high on foamy waves of oratory. [SS]

Our college football team was different: we didn't have a victory song—we had a song of surrender!

Our company's crack accountants took off their shoes so they could enlist their toes to help their fingers check the numbers.

Our leaders are addicted to doses of monetary morphine.

Raising teenagers is like nailing jello to a tree.

She clung onto him as desperately as kudzu.

She felt like she had just stepped into a BBC English saga.

She flashed a smile wider than the Grand Canyon.

She flitted from place to place like a hummingbird on steroids.

She gave him a look that would have raised the dead.

She was as disorganized as an overflowing laundry basket.

She's so thin, when she drinks cherry soda she looks like a thermometer.

When my friends found out that I was into meditation my popularity shot up—like Apple's stock. [VJ]

That idea is the unthinkable in pursuit of the impossible.

That was a Category Five lie ...

That's a sure ticket to patched pants and a bouncing bank account.

The situation turned into an airline counter after a flight cancellation.

The workday passed like molasses.

Their purses were shut tighter than Tupperware.

Their State bird is the mosquito.

There are more than a few milligrams of arrogance in him. [RJH]

When asked his opinion of New Zealand, the traveler replied: Hard to say—when I was there, it seemed to be shut.

My boss was huddled in his mahogany-lined foxhole.

The world is now so complex, if Moses came down from Mount Sinai today he wouldn't be carrying two tablets of stone but two tablets of valium.

Our situation is so absurd, so surreal, even Salvador Dali wouldn't understand it.

We have more lobbyists than grains in a sack of rice. [BHP]

We speak real slow here in the South—this speech usually takes about a month!

West Virginia: two million people and only 15 last names.

You need a checkup from the neck up to eliminate stinking thinking and prevent hardening of the attitudes. [ZZ]

## Exaggeration

I enjoyed that speech—although I was sorry to miss seeing my children grow up. <sup>SA</sup>

They were impulsive collectors—their home looked like a miniature Pharaoh's burial chamber for the living.

He was so unassuming, he was like a zero with the rim rubbed out.

He took off like a scalded cat on amphetamines <sup>RJH</sup>

When I came to breakfast singing that song my mom would light up like fireworks on the 4th of July. <sup>RJH</sup>

Now picture the gestures that went with this exaggeration-rich vignette—
*I look in my rear-view window and here's this guy—*
*He's road raging*
*He's honking*
*He's flashing his lights*
*He's waving his hands.*
*I was under control—*
*I did not flip him off.*
*I said—"You're not going to ruin my day."*
*All of a sudden I hear this clunk—and the truck moves.*
*I think—this idiot just ran into me.*
*I look in my side-view mirror just as my left rear tire passes me.*
*It missed the white station wagon coming down the road – it swerved.*
*Unfortunately, it took out Steinhower's mailbox.*
*It went down just like Kansas corn.* <sup>RJH</sup>

# Part II

# Humor Help for Chairmen

## Chair—For All Events

| | |
|---|---|
| Introduction & explanation | 109 |
| Opening the meeting or event | 110 |
| About the meeting | 112 |
| Quips to use as and when appropriate | 113 |
| Ending the meeting | 114 |
| Speaking and speeches | 115 |
| Speakers | 118 |
| Introducing speakers | 119 |
| Fun after-speech comments | 122 |
| Encouraging speech appreciation | 122 |
| Connecting comments with the audience | 123 |
| Verse and worse for all audiences | 131 |

## Chair—For Toastmaster Events

| | |
|---|---|
| Introduction & explanation | 133 |
| The organization | 134 |
| Speaking | 135 |
| Speeches | 135 |
| The speakers | 136 |
| Our club | 137 |
| Words | 138 |
| Longtime members | 138 |
| Others | 139 |
| Connecting comments with the audience | 140 |
| Me | 142 |
| Verse and worse for Toastmaster audiences | 143 |

# Chair: For All Events

Through our participation in business, church, civic, service, and charitable organizations, it is common to be invited to chair a large meeting of some form. The formal part of the meeting is usually laid out in the agenda. That's the easy part.

But when we seek ideas for the informal, lighthearted side of the meeting it's not so easy. Yes, we can go to a bookstore and buy Henny Youngman's *10,000 One Liners* or E. C. McKenzie's *14,000 Quips and Quotes*. Two great books but, alone, they don't provide a ready range of quips focused on chairing large meetings and conferences.

I have yet to find such a trusty guide so this section of chairmen's wit from many, many sources is offered to partially fill that gap. It's a simple list that has worked for me as I've prepared to chair meetings, and even draw from when preparing keynote speeches. As you read the collection, you'll discover quips with regional references (eg, Southern humor.) Obviously, these are not meant to offend, but to exemplify, and should be adapted or changed for whichever part of the world in which you live.

What I have learned about meeting quips is that there are two types: a general category that applies to most meetings, and a special category suitable for an organization with its unique vernacular. As a reader of this book, it's likely you belong to an organization with its special lingo. I do. Toastmasters. I joined over 50 years ago.

This chapter, All Events, covers the general category, and provides material to help you create smiles and laughter and more closely connect you with your audience when next you are chairman of almost any conference.

The chapter that follows uses Toastmasters as an example of a special category.

To assist in your search for the right quip, they are sorted into clusters:

- Opening the meeting or event
- About the meeting
- Quips to use as and when appropriate
- Ending the meeting
- Speaking and speeches
- Speakers
- Introducing speakers
- Fun after-speech comments
- Encouraging speech appreciation
- Connecting comments with the audience
- Verse and worse for all audiences

## Opening the meeting or event

Well friends, here I am! Now, what were your other two wishes?

Thank you for that very warm welcome. Your applause was almost enough to make me feel humble—almost!

Thank you for coming. If it wasn't for all of you, I'd be here all alone.

Gentlemen, if you love Southern women, raise your glasses. If you don't—raise your standards. [WS+]

Look around. You women here tonight look so beautiful, it's sad to think that in 20 years, you'll all be 10 years older. [~GJ]

It was hard to get up at 4:00 this morning to get here—although it didn't really bother me after the alarm rang for the third time. [VF]

Welcome to our typical Conference—where the average IQ is lower than our average age.

Our Annual Conference is a special event—THIS is where fun comes to be rejuvenated!

People come to conventions like this because you just can't hug old friends or shake hands with new ones over the phone or on Facebook.

A conference is just an admission that you want somebody to join you in your troubles—I mean, just look around! WR

How are y'all tonight? Your usual self? Wonderful! I'm my usual self, too—depressed, moody, irritable, rude. Apart from that, I'm looking forward to a great meeting.

[If the meeting attendance is low]: Wow! You must be a very wealthy crowd. I see you have bought two or three seats each! ~CW

Let me begin by reciting the Chairman's Prayer: *Just for today Lord, keep your arm around my shoulder and your hand over my mouth.*

The duty of a chairman or emcee is to be so dull that all the speakers appear brilliant in contrast. You'll be relieved to know I'm planning to play my part. CBK

You're all so lucky! Today is my Annual Smart Day! You're in for a great meeting!

Today, out of respect for my friends, I shall try to keep my charisma in check.

There's no need to treat me any differently than you would a King (or Queen).

I would like to say a few words. — Now, if you believe that, you'll believe anything.

## About the meeting

We hope you are going to hear many great speeches tonight. Of course, we can't guarantee that. In fact, we can't guarantee anything anymore. For example, we can't even guarantee the quality of the 100% Extra Virgin Olive Oil on your salad—how would we know if a couple of olives had ever decided to stray?

Ladies and Gentlemen, tonight you are under no obligation to laugh. However, if you don't, we have a brand-new audience warming up in the basement. [JD]

Laugh alone and the world thinks you're an idiot. So, tonight, let's laugh out loud together and prove them wrong.

I don't mind if people go to sleep while I'm talking—but I do mind if you don't say goodnight first.

We received a number of congratulatory messages for this event—from people congratulating themselves for not being here. [FC]

## Quips to use as and when appropriate

There's no joke at the end of this, so if you want to laugh, you might want to start now.

I know what I'm saying—I just don't know what you're hearing. [MA+]

I'm sure you're aware of the latest Mayo Clinic findings—your body doesn't absorb cholesterol if taken from another person's plate—so go ahead and enjoy your dinner!

Let's take a 5-minute break—or else we'll have a 10-minute unscheduled loss of control.

We are at a significant point in our program—it's time for lunch.

As the toastmaster, it's my job to tell you that the best part of the dinner is now over.

My friends, I shall be brief—no matter how long it takes.

Unaccustomed as I am to speaking in public—for free!

I won't talk long — I'm a short speaker.

Understand that my job is just to introduce the speakers—not to guarantee them. [HY]

Our meeting rules are simple. First allow me to finish speaking. Then you can interrupt.

Yes, I know that the food is awful tonight—and that there's not enough of it!

Oliver Wendell Holmes believed that a mind stretched by a new idea never reverts to its original shape. I hope your mind is ready for some great exercise today.

## Ending the meeting

We look forward to seeing y'all again at our next Conference. If you're not here with us, then I'll expect to see your name in the Obituary notices. [HC^]

"In conclusion" — Don't you love that phrase? It's like a wake-up call to the audience.

I think I'll just put an "Out of Order" sticker on my forehead and call it a day.

And now, in response to numerous requests, the meeting is adjourned.

## Speaking, speeches, and speakers

The human mind is unbelievable. It starts working even before we are born. And works continuously 24 hours a day collecting and storing information, and never stops until we [pause] stand up to give a speech. [HP^]

No one has ever complained about a speech being too short! [IH]

It seems that some presenters have mastered the art of speaking—without disclosing what they are talking about.

Light travels faster than sound. Did you know that's the reason why some people appear bright—until you hear them speak?

Speaking is all about honesty, and if you can fake that, you've got it made. [GB]

Speakers should never confuse the seating capacity of the auditorium with the sitting capacity of the audience.

The three Big B's of speaking are: Be brief. Be interesting. Be gone. [VS]

When the speaker doesn't boil it down, the audience has to sweat it out. [RD+]

Remember that speaking is NOT the art of making deep sounds in the chest, thinking they are important messages from the brain.

A good speech is like a comet—dazzling, eye-opening, and over before you know it.

A speaker is one who is invited to give a few words but doesn't know when to stop. [CW]

An after-dinner speaker is someone asked to say a few words—but then says too many.

An after-dinner speaker is the person who starts the "bull" rolling. [HY]

A speech is like a love affair. Any fool can start it—ending it, however, requires considerable skill. [LM>]

Every speaker has his moment—the problem is that most stretch it into an hour. [CW]

Have you noticed some speakers don't know very much, but they sure say it fluently? [HR]

Speeches are like babies—easy to conceive, hard to deliver. [PO]

Some speeches are like boiled lobster. You have to pick through an awful lot before you find the meat. ~EM

Sometimes, it seems that a speaker's biggest challenge is to get his mouth and mind synchronized.

The best speech is one that has a great beginning, a memorable end, and not much in between. CW

The easiest way to stay awake during an after-dinner speech is to deliver it. EM

The mark of a good keynote speaker is the ability to say nothing—briefly.

The problem with some speakers is you can't hear what they're saying. The problem with others is that you can.

The secret of a good speech is to have a good beginning and a good ending—and to have the two as close together as possible. GB

A person gushed to Earl Nightingale after hearing him speak: "I want to be a great speaker like you some day." Earl politely asked: "And what is it that you want to say?"

The shortest distance between two points is rarely found in speeches.

There are two types of speakers—those who are nervous and those who are liars. [MT]

One good speaking rule is that if your mind ever goes blank don't forget to turn off the sound. [HR]

Your speech need not be eternal to be immortal—Muriel Humphrey once quietly counseled her loquacious husband, Vice President Hubert Humphrey.

## Speakers

A Spanish proverb tells us not to speak unless we can improve upon the silence. You'll be reassured that all our speakers tonight have committed to meet that goal.

Alfred E. Neuman told us: "Some minds are like concrete—all mixed up and permanently set." Let's hope none of those minds are here tonight as our guest speaker will shortly be turning on our mental concrete mixers.

Craig Valentine tells us that the biggest room in the world is the room for improvement. Tonight, our speaker will be sharing with us some ways to fill that room.

I don't mind how long our speakers talk—as long they say it in a few words.

## Introducing speakers

It's my pleasure to introduce our after-dinner speaker—the "gust" of honor.

I shall avoid repeating what one Chairman said to their distinguished speaker: "Should we let them enjoy themselves a little longer—or should we have your speech now?" ~JL>

One of the requirements of the meeting Chair is to be sensitive, and not be like the one who gushed: "You were so much better than our last speaker. He spoke for an hour and never said anything. You took only 15 minutes." ~DB+

Our featured speaker needs no introduction—he's sick and couldn't make it. HR

Tonight, I'd like to introduce a man with unbelievable charm, talent, and wit. Unfortunately, we couldn't find one, so instead let me introduce...

Our speaker today is special: each speech he gives is always better than his next.

We have a few minutes to kill and I don't know anyone who can kill time better than our next speaker. Let's give him a warm welcome... JN^

Our next speaker has a 10-minute speech—but it will take 30 minutes to deliver.

We are delighted to have our next speaker with us. He meets our two standard requirements: he believes in free speech and—he believes in free speeches.

Our next speaker always gives speeches that please everyone. Those who agree with them, think them over—and those who don't, are glad they're over.

Our next speaker has been married so long, he and his wife are on their fourth bottle of Tabasco!

Our next speaker is a man of many convictions who, fortunately, has not done time for any of them. [DB+]

Our next speaker is one who does things on a grand scale—his house is so big it's even got its own zip code.

Our next speaker is so active when speaking he generates enough energy for ET to phone home.

Our next speaker is so persuasive he could sell a muzzle to a dog.

Our next speaker is so smart he discovered a cure for which there is no disease. [VB]

Our next speaker is so smart that sometimes even he doesn't understand a single word of what he is saying. ~OW

Our next speaker knows the guidelines. He may speak as long as he likes—as long as he finishes early.

Our next speaker needs no introduction—although I hope he brought a conclusion. HR

Our next speaker works for a great company—they have Margarita Mondays, Wired Wednesdays, and TGIF Fridays.

Our next speaker has about as many money worries as Warren Buffet.

We've told our speakers that we don't care how long they speak—provided it's said in a few words.

There are two types of speakers—those who never stop to think and those who never think to stop. Fortunately, our next speaker doesn't fall into either category...

Malcolm Muggeridge observed that only dead fish swim with the stream. You will soon discover that our next speaker is definitely not a dead fish.

## Fun after-speech comments

My colleague has covered the ground well with his remarks. What he's covered it with I don't know—but there should be a bumper crop next year!

Remember that monotone is the first two-thirds of monotonous. [BH^]

He's a remarkable man. He knows exactly where he's going and where he's been—he's just not quite sure where he is right now. [~MM]

The speaker surely had style—he even yawned during his own speech.

May the gnats of a thousand camels settle in your armpits to thank you for your challenging speech today.

Those words were very impressive—well above my pay-grade.

## Encouraging speaker appreciation

I'm hearing a lot of loud one-handed clapping. Now let's put both hands together.

Let's put our hands together to welcome our next speaker to the lectern ...

## Connecting comments with the audience

Friends—excuse me, but I know you all too well to call you Ladies and Gentlemen—

For our younger attendees, let me tell you that YES, you are in the right place, and NO, even though it might seem like it, this is NOT an AARP meeting. <sup>AN</sup>

Don't worry if the meeting starts getting dull—oxygen masks will automatically fall from the ceiling.

I sense your excitement. All of us are younger today than we will ever be again! ~EP^

Don't you just love audience involvement? Recently I was giving a speech at a Conference when a fellow at the back shouted: *I can't hear you.* Then a fellow up front shouted: *I can —let's trade seats!*

Audiences usually comprise two groups: those who agree with you—and bigots. <sup>EM</sup>

Now, back in the days when our ties were wider and our waists were thinner...

Don't you just love how modern technology amplifies our voices so clearly? I'm hoping someone will invent a machine that will amplify our ideas just as clearly.

Haven't you noticed how some people create happiness wherever they go and some people create happiness whenever they go? RBZ

Keep your dream alive—hit the snooze button.

Don't you talk to yourself? I do—where else should I go for expert advice?

Well, it seems unanimous that we cannot agree.

The greatest after-dinner speech I've ever heard was, "I'll take the check."

Thank you for that sitting ovation.

The speaker talked a lot but said nothing.

You might be thinking—What's his point? [Pause] Well, thanks for asking. My point is...

I hope this doesn't describe us. — A conference is a place where everybody talks, nobody listens, and everybody disagrees afterwards. EM

Take my advice — I'm not using it. [FC]

The two most beautiful words in the English language are "Check Enclosed." [DP]

Things were so quiet — I knew he must have just cracked a joke.

*Two roads diverged in a wood and I—I took the one less travelled by.* Did you know that Robert Frost's great poem has been updated by the Millennials? *Two roads diverged in a wood and I—I took the one less tweeted about.*

Our next speaker needs no introduction—certainly not the extravaganza he gave me to read to you. [~GP]

Economists have discovered that talk is cheap because supply exceeds demand.

I hope you're happy today. If you're not, which day will you choose to be?

Aren't parents so logical? They want their kids to be normal—but above average.

Ever feel life's too short—need an extra day inserted between Saturday and Sunday?

Do promise to go to your company Christmas Party this year—it's a great opportunity to catch up with people you haven't seen for a couple of hours!

There are only seven days in the week and "someday" isn't one of them—so when exactly is it you're going to start working on your next goal?

Blame your kids on your parents—if they didn't have kids, you wouldn't either.

He's so old his Social Security number is 1.

He's so old there are rocks named after him.

He's so old there are rocks younger than him.

I'd sing for you, but I don't want the meeting to end early.

I'm retired. I was tired yesterday. I'm tired again today.

That was a great speech. Those of us who are still awake salute you. ~PW

We searched high and low for an interesting speaker for tonight—we found our next speaker during the low part of the search. GP

I've been looking forward to this occasion with mixed emotions—terror and fear.

I've never forgotten the first time I spoke in front of a big crowd. The speaker before me was so bad, they booed him three times—it was embarrassing—they even booed him during my presentation! BH^

It's always darkest just before dawn. So, if you're going to steal your neighbor's newspaper, that's the time to do it. BH^

Now let's get back to where I was before I rudely interrupted myself.

Now listen up y'all—I have nothing to say and I'm only going to say it once. So be alert. All right, first question—hands up if you know what a lert is.

He speaks fast. Can crack six jokes in a minute—that's because he never has to stop for laughs. ~PW

Let's now take this moment to talk about someone with great talent, great personality, and great charm. Unfortunately, we can't, as we aren't here to talk about me.

Okay, everyone, it's that time when we light the incense and start the chanting.

Once I was so far back in the hall, the speech seemed more like a rumor.

Dale Carnegie told us one way to ensure an effective delivery is to look your audience straight in the eyes and speak as if every one of them owed you money.

Advice is like castor oil—easy to give, but dreadful to take. [JB+]

If you're like me, you don't need another To Do List—you need a Stop Doing List.

Marcel Proust believed the only real voyage of discovery is not in seeking new landscapes but in having new eyes. Let's hope we all gain new eyes tonight.

A conference is the confusion of one man multiplied by the number present. [EM]

We've all had this experience—we've stood up but then our voice stood down.

Don't worry about the world ending today. It's already tomorrow in New Zealand.

A conference is a gathering of important people who singly can do nothing but, together, can decide that nothing can be done. FA

I could say many nice things about our next speaker, but I'd rather be honest. GP

I could listen to you forever. And I think I just did.

Let me also comment on the speaker's handsome suit: it's a real tribute to the quality of the cloth, the skill of the tailor—and the generosity of the Salvation Army. ~PW

[In response to a flattering Introduction] You spoke so flatteringly about me I thought for a moment I was dead. HST

Think seriously about this one—if you have a net worth greater than zero, you are wealthier than the US Government.

He wasted no words in his speech—he used every single one of them. [SA]

Let's give our next speaker a great hand—it may be the only one he gets tonight. [GP]

I am extremely pleased to introduce a man who is so clever and witty—and I could go on and on and on—but I'm having terrible trouble reading his handwriting. [~PW]

Voltaire said, "Light your candle at every man's torch." Let me assure you, our speaker tonight will soon have all your candles burning brightly…

Even Shakespeare knew the secret of speaking. He told us: "Men of few words are the best men."

Churchill, known for his oratory, once described a good speech as being like a woman's skirt—long enough to cover the subject and short enough to create interest.

The role of toastmaster relative to the speaker is that of the fan to the fan dancer—to draw attention to the subject, without trying to cover it. [AS]

Some people talk a lot but say nothing —I see my wife eyeing me—which tells me it's time to stop saying nothing.

## Verse and Worse for Any Event

**There are three types of attendees here tonight—**
The gossip who talks about others
The bore who talks about himself
And the conversationalist who talks about you.
May we all be great conversationalists tonight.


**Ode to a Speaker (with apologies to John Keats)—**
Oh, I love a finished speaker
I really, really do.
I don't mean one who's polished
I mean one who's really through. ~JL>


**Before we discuss business matters—**
**Let's remember what a committee is ...**
A committee is a collection of the unfit
Chosen from the unwilling
By the incompetent
To do the unnecessary. AN


**Some advice before we begin—**
Beware of speakers on programs
Who stick to the lectern like glue
They warm to their subject by saying
"I could go on and on" —
And then unfortunately do. AN


**There are three rules of speaking—**
To be seen one must stand up
To be heard one must speak up
To be appreciated one must sit down. VS

# Chair: For Toastmaster Events

Toastmasters® was founded in 1924 with the motto: *Better Listening. Better Thinking. Better Speaking.* From one embryonic club, it has grown into a global organization with clubs in over 140 countries, providing a forum for all who wish to learn and develop speaking skills, prepare and deliver better speeches, and connect more effectively. Each year, it hosts an International Speech Contest to find that year's World Champion of Public Speaking® (WCPS). To find nearby club locations, go to www.Toastmasters.org and click "Find a Club."

The quips, quotes, and one-liners in this chapter are designed to help when you are the chairperson of a Toastmasters meeting, contest, or conference, or even when a speaker at a Toastmaster function. They are offered as a starter kit, to be quoted, used, or adapted. This separate section was created because its contents and lingo may not be fully understood by non-Toastmasters. That said, many of the entries can readily be "translated" and adapted for use in other organizations such as Rotary, Kiwanis, and Lions.

The quips and quotes are clustered into the following sections:

- The organization
- Speaking
- Speeches
- The speakers
- Our club
- Words
- Longtime members
- Others
- Connecting comments with the audience
- Me
- Verse and Worse for Toastmaster audiences

## The organization

If you get out of Toastmasters all you can get out of Toastmasters—you'll never get out of Toastmasters ... Helen Blanchard, first female President of Toastmasters

I am not in Toastmasters. Toastmasters is in me.

Toastmasters takes us on a journey from stage fright to stage delight.

Robert Frost told us, *Half the world has nothing to say, and keep saying it. The other half has something to say and doesn't.* — The purpose of Toastmasters is to help both halves.

`

I don't know what brought you to Toastmasters but I do know where it can take you. [DW>]

Any Toastmaster who doesn't get involved beyond his club is like someone who goes no further than the salad bar—he's missing out on the main course. [BH^]

Don't let it be said of you: *He was a phantom member—he left no fingerprints on his club.*

No one comes to Toastmasters just to be a better speaker at Toastmasters. We come to be better speakers outside of our club, too. [DLC]

## Speaking

Advice to new speakers: if you don't know what to talk about—talk about three minutes.

Be encouraged by Ralph Waldo Emerson's observation: Few speakers are born with speaking skills—all the great speakers were bad speakers first.

Don't speak too long. It's best to leave your audience before your audience leaves you.

Can you believe some people speak for an hour without notes—or even without a point!!

Speaker's advice: The more funny — the more money. EF^

Toastmaster's advice: if you haven't struck oil within five minutes—stop boring.

## Speeches

Years ago, I confessed to a wise old speaker that I didn't know where to begin. His helpful reply—Near the end.

If you can't write your message in a sentence, you won't be able to give it in an hour. ~DB+

Mark Twain said that it usually took him more than three weeks to prepare a good impromptu speech. In Toastmasters, we're better than that. We prepare great speeches in the car on the way to the meeting!

A great speech is often education wrapped in entertainment. [DR^]

A good speech is like a good pot of soup—it gets better when you reheat it.

Stories open your audience's hearts—their wallets often follow.

In Toastmasters, we learn that a conclusion is the place where we get tired of thinking. So let me close now by saying...

## The speakers

Our speaker will appreciate your indulgence today. He is working on the Longhorn speech assignment. That's the one with two widely-separated points—with a lot of bull in between. [BH^]

Our speaker lineup today is so compelling I am not expecting any of them will be sitting down to a thunderous lack of interest.

Her speeches are like pizza—even the worst ones are great!

## Our club

To get us all in the right mood, we're going to start our meeting with 15 seconds of your greatest fake laughing.

Our club has found a creative way to screen new members—they don't qualify until they laugh at a joke of our Club President—even though it may take awhile.

To qualify as a joke at Toastmasters, it must be really good or really bad. I'm pleased to say that your joke today qualified.

This member has brought a lot to our club—mostly room for improvement. [JN]

In this club, when giving evaluations we avoid soliloquys of whitewash—those are left to Tom Sawyer and Huck Finn. [TK]

We want our evaluations to be so good that our club number will be carved on the face of Feedback Mountain.

Our club's Contest Judges are as inscrutable as a roulette wheel.

I've never had so much fun with my clothes on as I have in my club. [BH]

## Words

I've never forgotten the date I had with one Toastmaster. At its end, she looked me in the eye and, without dangling a participle or splitting an infinitive, she told me to straighten up, get a life, and get lost. I was truly impressed—with that triple she delivered.

In Toastmasters, we learn the importance and value of words. For example, we learn that the five most expensive words in the English language are: *You may kiss the bride.*

I lost my mother when I was 3—I found her an hour later in a different part of the Mall. [Pause] Which reminds us that in Toastmasters we must be very careful with the meaning of every word we use.

## Longtime members

He's been a Toastmaster a long time—long before Alexander became Great.

He's been a Toastmaster a long time—long before cavemen were herding dinosaurs.

He's been a Toastmaster a long, long time—long before Sears met Roebuck, before Rolls met Royce—before Harry met Sally.

He's been here so long, he deserves to have his face carved on Mount Toastmore.

## Others

His sense of humor had been surgically removed before he joined Toastmasters—we're happy to report, however, it's now been fully restored!

I hear that Bluegrass singer Alison Krauss is a Toastmaster. Her pauses give her away. Remember her line … *You say it best—when you say nothing at all?*

Every World Champion will tell you that the Contest standard has declined ever since the year he or she won! ᴰᴿ^

Have you ever noticed that some speakers seem to take a connecting flight to get where they think they're going?

He has the true Toastmasters religion. He's a devout disciple. He rattles the windows, rocks the rafters, and exhorts members to jump up and shout: Praise the Verb! Glorify the Grammarian! Hallelujah to the Hot Seat! ᴮᵂ

He's so hyper he's like an anxiety-driven noun in search of a sweet, lonely verb.

When you speak, you're like E. F. Hutton—we all listen.

He speaks like a man who is out of practice of being wrong.

## Connecting comments with the audience

Friends, please don't knock the coffee today. You may be old and weak someday too!

Let me read you something, if I may. Even if I may not, I'll read it anyway.

Toastmasters are unique. They are so unbelievably supportive, they applaud everything — even blades of grass when they see grass growing.

That was a toast-worthy performance.

Now that speech was supposed to make us roll over on our backs with all four paws in the air...

That speech probably sounded better in the original German.

I've practiced this speech all week and feel pretty good about it. So, if you could just manage to look more like my bathroom mirror, I'll begin...

Are you one of the many Toastmasters who dream of one day becoming a hired tongue?

If there was a contest for speech titles, I'd nominate my favorite country song: *How Can I Miss You When You Won't Go Away?*

Some older club members believe DTM stands for Don't Time Me.

There are three kinds of speakers: winners, losers, and those who write telling the second group how the first group succeeded.

Ever had a club meeting in the cemetery? It's a great place to make it come alive.

I feel like a ginsu-knife salesman up here with all these props.

When General Evaluator, do you ever feel like Congressman Trey Gowdy's three dogs, whose names are Judge, Jury, and Bailiff?

What's the difference between a cat and a comma? — One has claws at the end of its paws, and one is a pause at the end of a clause. ~SL

Now where was I before I interrupted myself?

## Me

I have a confession to make. I'm a convicted bigamist—I'm married to two Toastmaster clubs and currently having an affair with another one out of town.

Excuse me, but I am a recovering Toastaholic.

I have been in Toastmasters so long I was actually here when the calendar switched from BC to AD. Yes, I actually walked this planet both Before Computers and After Dell.

I practice my speeches in front of my wife—which is okay—apart from her convulsive laughter.

I was recently approached by the President to be our country's Ambassador to Toastmania (not to confused with Tasmania in Australia) — that huge body of people in over 140 countries identified as Toastmasters, Toastaholics, and Speechaholics.

When I became a Toastmasters, my wife thought I was joining a cult—she was right!

I've been a Toastmaster for a number of years—that number is (give #).

I have left instructions that my tombstone read: Here lies Brian Woolf. Toastaholic. Had lots more to say—but the red light came on.

## Verse and Worse for Toastmaster Events

**Our leadership team has a new mantra—**
We the unwilling
Led by the unknowing—
Are doing the impossible
For the ungrateful—
And have done so much
For so long
With so little—
We are now qualified
To do anything
With nothing. ᴬᴺ

**Recently, there was a big "survey" about the risks of dating a Toastmaster. Here were some of the men's comments—**

- Dinner conversations with her were interrupted by a green, yellow, and red light.
- The first time I visited her home I got a five-minute tour of her trophy shelf.
- Her refrigerator was covered with Best Speaker ribbons.
- She evaluated everything I said.

**And some of the women's comments—**

- When he first asked me for a date, it took him 5-7 minutes to get to the point.
- I thought he owned a ship in Greenland because he kept talking about how people loved his Icebreaker.
- When visiting famous landmarks, he takes selfies while holding a Toastmasters magazine.
- He flinched every time I said Um or Ah.

## Some Comments Heard from Chairmen Prior to Announcing Contest Results:

I have a peculiar feeling that this must be what hell is like [while awaiting the Judges' results]. Here I am standing in front of 400 people and I can't say a word!

Here's the envelope we've all been waiting for. [Open … pause] It reads … *The results will be ready tomorrow!* … Oops! I misread that… *our 3rd place winner is …*

Here's the news you've all been waiting for. [Pause] *We are having chicken for dinner!* [Pause—then the Chair moves on to announce the judges' results.]

# Superscripts Index

Note: If a tilde (~) precedes a listed superscript (eg, ~MT), the original quote selected has been adapted to make it shorter or clearer. Symbols after initials (eg, DW^, DW+, and DW>) are used to differentiate people with the same initials.

The term WCPS attached to some names below denotes Toastmasters® World Champion of Public Speaking®. Some winners also use the term World Champion Speaker.

| | | | |
|---|---|---|---|
| AB^ | Aaron Beverly | DS^ | Dwayne Smith WCPS |
| AL | Abraham Lincoln | DS> | David Sanfacon |
| AM | Lord Arthur Milverton | DT^ | Darren Tay Wen Jie WCPS |
| AN | Anonymous | DW^ | Diana Watson |
| AP^ | Alan Parham | DW+ | Dan Weedin |
| AS | Adlai Stevenson | DW> | Douglas Wilson |
| AW | Art Woo | EB | Erma Bombeck |
| BB | Bill Bonner | EBW | E B White |
| BC | Bennett Cerf | EEC | e e cummings |
| BH^ | Bob Herndon | EF^ | Eric Feinendegen |
| BHP | Brian Picot | EH^ | Ed Hearn WCPS |
| BM | Bette Midler | EM | E C McKenzie |
| BM^ | Bill Mintz | EMM | Ed McManus |
| BM+ | Bill Murray | EP^ | Evelyn Payton |
| BML | Beverly McLaughlin | ET^ | Ed Tate WCPS |
| BR^ | Brett Rutledge WCPS | FA | Fred Allen |
| BW | Brian Woolf | FC | Friars Club |
| CB^ | Cliff Boer | GB | George Burns |
| CBD | Cecil B De Mille | GF | Gerald Ford |
| CBK | Clarence B Kelland | GH | Gordie Howe |
| CG | Carol Gregory | GHB | George H W Bush |
| CM | Christopher Myers | GHP | George Herbert Palmer |
| CV^ | Craig Valentine WCPS | GJ | George Jessel |
| CW | Canuwrite.com | GM | Groucho Marx |
| CW+ | Carrie Warren | GN | Greenville News |
| DB | Dave Bricker | GO | George Orwell |
| DB+ | James "Doc" Blakely | GP | Gene Perret |
| DB> | Daach'ana Blaydes | HC^ | Helen Cash |
| DH^ | Dananjaya Hettiarachchi WCPS | HH | Herbert Hoover |
| DH+ | David Henderson WCPS | HK | Henry Kissinger |
| DK^ | Douglas Kruger | HP^ | Harold Patterson WCPS |
| DLC | Darren LaCroix WCPS | HR | Hal Roach |
| DM+ | Don Marquis | HST | Harry S Truman |
| DMM | Don McMillan | HY | Henny Youngman |
| DN^ | David Nottage WCPS | IH | Ira Hayes |
| DP | Dorothy Parker | JA^ | Jonathan Abuyan |
| DP^ | Dwight Pledger | JA> | John Andrews |
| DR^ | David Ross WCPS | JB | Jack Benny |

| | | | |
|---|---|---|---|
| JB^ | Jeremiah Bacon | MM^ | Morgan McArthur WCPS |
| JB+ | Josh Billings | MM+ | Margaret Mead |
| JB> | Jimmy Buffett | MQ^ | Mohammed Qahtani WCPS |
| JD | Jimmy Durante | MR+ | Manie Robinson |
| JD^ | Joel Dawson | MT | Mark Twain |
| JE^ | Jock Elliott WCPS | MV^ | Manoj Vasudevan WCPS |
| JF | Jeff Foxworthy | MW+ | Mae West |
| JG | John Glenn | MW | Marie Woolf |
| JG^ | Joseph Grondin | NQ | Nido Qubein |
| JK^ | Jim Key WCPS | ON | Ogden Nash |
| JL | Jay Leno | OW | Oscar Wilde |
| JL^ | Josephine Lee | P | Plato |
| JL> | Justin Lee | PD | Phyllis Diller |
| JM^ | Jason Malham | PF | Patricia Fripp |
| JM> | Jean MacDonald | PH | Patricia Hill |
| JN | Joe Namath | PK | Paul Keating |
| JN^ | Jay Nodine | PO | Pat O'Malley |
| JN> | Jack Nicholson | PS^ | Palaniappa Subramaniam |
| JP | Joe Pasquale | PW | Pat Williams |
| JR | Joan Rivers | RA | Ron Atkinson |
| JR> | Jeanne Robertson | RA^ | Ryan Avery WCPS |
| JW^ | James Webb | RB | Robert J Burdette |
| JY^ | Jeff Young WCPS | RBZ | Roy B Zuck |
| KCG | K C Goh | RC | Raymond Chandler |
| KH^ | Katina Hunter | RD | Rodney Dangerfield |
| KK^ | Kim Kaufman | RD^ | Russ Dantu |
| KM^ | Kevin McCue | RD+ | Raymond Duncan |
| KS | Kelly Swanson | RF | Robert Frost |
| KYY | Kwong Yue Yan | RF^ | Roy Fenstermaker WCPS |
| LC^ | Linus Chang | RH^ | Rich Hopkins |
| LG | Sen. Lindsey Graham | RH= | Richard Hardon |
| LL^ | Larry Lands | RH> | Rolf Harris |
| LM^ | Lance Miller WCPS | RJ^ | Rita Joyan |
| LM> | Lord Mancroft | RJH | Randy J Harvey WCPS |
| LSR | LaShunda Rundles WCPS | RL | Russell Lynes |
| LT | Lana Turner | RMK | Robert Mackenzie |
| LT+ | Lily Tomlin | RO | Robert Orben |
| MA | Maureen Abdulla | RR^ | Rebecca Raglan |
| MA^ | Michael Aun WCPS | RR+ | Robert Redford |
| MA+ | Mike Atkin | RS^ | Richard Spencer |
| MH | Mitch Hedberg | RW | Ralph Walker |
| MH^ | Mark Hunter WCPS | SA | Stephen Arnott |
| MI | Molly Ivins | SB^ | Simon Bucknall |
| ML^ | Mario Lewis | SF | Sigmund Freud |
| MM | Mitch Murray | SG | Sam Goldwyn |

| | | | | |
|---|---|---|---|---|
| SH | Shady Hoffman | | VF | Valda Ford |
| SJ | Samuel Johnson | | VJ^ | Vikas Jhingran [WCPS] |
| SJ^ | Sherwood Jones | | VL | Vince Lombardi |
| SK^ | Sameera Khan | | VS | Various Sources |
| SL | Sam Leith | | WA | Woody Allen |
| SL^ | Susan Lamb | | WB | Warren Buffett |
| SS | Simon Schama | | WC | Winston Churchill |
| SS^ | Simon Scriver | | WCF | W C Fields |
| SW | Steven Wright | | WF | William Faulkner |
| TB^ | Terry Begue | | WJ^ | Willie Jones [WCPS] |
| TC+ | Terry Canfield | | WM^ | Will May |
| TC> | Ted Cruz | | WP^ | Will Powell |
| TG | Texas Guinan | | WR | Will Rogers |
| TG> | Tour Guide, St Petersburg | | WS+ | William Shearer |
| TK^ | Trent Kenelly | | YB | Yogi Berra |
| TS | T-Shirt or Bumper Sticker | | YC | You-can-be-funny.com |
| TW | TheNextWeb.com | | ZZ | Zig Ziglar |
| VB | Victor Borge | | | |

**Also available at Amazon.com**

"Brian Woolf got it right! He covers all the essentials in his book, *The Speaker's Toolbox*. If you want to be a powerful presenter, this book is full of ideas to help you. I wish this resource was around when I started. Well done!"

—Darren LaCroix, CSP, AS, World Champion Speaker

"Brian—Tremendous research! You clearly do have a passion for speeches. You've provided a book that will teach many for years to come!"

—Harold Patterson, World Champion Speaker

"I am impressed with your book. Great job! The useful tools you've included and the numerous speeches you've analyzed will be a blessing for every speaker."

—Presiyan Vasilev, World Champion Speaker

"I will require every one of my protégés to read this book. It lays out so succinctly the key elements that so many speakers struggle with, the things that are so hard to explain. I loved the combination of great minds and speakers outside Toastmasters as well as those within. The footnoting procedure is excellent. Thank you for this book!"

—Randy J Harvey, World Champion Speaker

# About the Author

**Brian Woolf** is a speechaholic. He loves listening to speeches, thinking about them, and giving them; and he loves reading and studying them— their makeup, their message, their music—to discover their magic.

It wasn't always so. In high school, he ardently avoided entering the annual speech contests. While at University he "bombed" with a speech at a major black-tie dinner. At 22, in his first job, he knew he needed speaking help. Toastmasters clubs were just being introduced to his native New Zealand. He joined. He learned. He gained speaking confidence ... enough to subsequently use the skills learned to graduate with Distinction from Harvard Business School with its two-year program of dialogue-based case studies. In later years, he has spoken extensively, including to conferences on five continents.

Toastmasters' plays a key part in his life. Brian has been an active member in clubs in New Zealand, Ireland, and six States in the USA. Besides earning its highest award, Distinguished Toastmaster (DTM), he has won six District (State) Speech Contests— and lost many more (which is when the intensive learning occurs!) In 2003, he was one of nine finalists in Toastmasters World Championship of Public Speaking®.

Mastering communication skills has helped him not only at Toastmasters but also in the business world and as an author.

## Comments and suggestions

Should you know of any quotation attributed in this book with an older pedigree, I would appreciate learning of it. Likewise, if you care to share any comments or suggestions, or have any quotations you think worthy of inclusion in a future reprint or website posting, please send them to:

*brianwoolf@speakers-toolbox.com*

## For more information

Visit: *www.speakers-toolbox.com*

Made in the USA
Middletown, DE
26 February 2024